Jesus and Politics

José María Casciaro

FOUR COURTS PRESS

This book is a translation by Michael Adams of
Jesucristo y la sociedad politica (Ediciones Palabra,
S.A., Madrid 1973); it was typeset in Ireland in 11 on
12pt Baskerville IBM.

ISBN 0 906127 63 7 cased
ISBN 0 906127 64 5 paperback

Nihil obstat: Stephen J Greene, censor deputatus.
Imprimi potest: Dermot Archbishop of Dublin,.
22 June 1983. (The Nihil obstat and Imprimi potest
are a declaration that a book or publication is considered to be free from doctrinal or moral error. This
declaration does not imply approval of, or agreement
with, the contents, opinions or statements expressed.)

Printed in Ireland

British Library Cataloguing in Publication Data

Casciaro, José Maria
  Jesus and politics.
  1. Jesus Christ
  2. Christianity and politics
  I. Title   II. Adams, Michael
  III. Jesucristo y la sociedad politica. *English*
  232.9'01   BT590.P/

  ISBN 0-906127-64-5
  ISBN 0-906127-63-7 Pbk

Jesus and Politics

CONTENTS

A preliminary observation

It is quite impossible to restrict the personality of Jesus Christ within a merely human framework: it breaks all moulds. This is what happens when we try in a 'scientific way' to focus on one particular aspect of Jesus' life, presenting him as teacher, prophet, Messiah or Son of God: our previous ideas about what these roles involved begin to blur and merge with one another: they will not stay in place.

We all know this very well. By pointing to this rich personality of Jesus and our inability to grasp it fully, I simply want to say that this essay is necessarily incomplete. I hope that I will show clearly that Jesus Christ, in his public ministry, acted in an essentially and exclusively religious way, and yet, no man ever had — no man has! — such an impact on purely human and even 'temporal' affairs as Jesus Christ did. But this latter aspect is not what concerns us here; I simply want to say that I am very aware of the limited focus of this essay.

Introduction

Pilate also wrote a title and put it on the cross; it read, "Jesus of Nazareth, the King of the Jews". Many of the Jews read this title, for the place where Jesus was crucified was near the city; and it was written in Hebrew, in Latin, and in Greek. The chief priests of the Jews then said to Pilate, "Do not write, 'The King of the Jews', but, 'This man said, I am the King of the Jews'". Pilate answered, "what I have written I have written" (Jn 19:19-22).

This notice put on the cross was not an invention of the procurator; it was standard Roman practice in cases of capital punishment: the grounds for the sentence were posted on the cross. The technical name for this notice was *titulus*[1], a term retained by St John in his Greek transcription *titlon* (Jn 19:19). As St Matthew put it: "And over his head they put the charge against him, which read, 'This is Jesus, the King of the Jews'" (Mt 27:37). The interesting thing is that the content of the *titulus* in the specific case of Jesus was a purely political crime.

In terms of Roman law, it amounted to this: Jesus of Nazareth has been condemned to death and executed by crucifixion because he is guilty of political subversion and state security in this province of the Empire must be maintained.[2]

What I propose to do now is look at Jesus' trial and at the circumstances in which it took place — seeing it not as a historical curiosity but as a paradigm of a drama which keeps being played out in the experience of Jesus' mystical body, the Church.

Israel, as a people and a nation, was at that time under the political control of Gentiles. It has lost its independence although, in keeping with the Roman system, it had been allowed a certain autonomy for certain internal affairs: this autonomy affected its religious institutions.[3] But this fell very far short of its national and specially its politico-religious ideal: Israel aimed at being a special theocracy; theocracy was rooted in its centuries-old history.

It was difficult for the Roman governors (as it is for any new-to-the-subject historian) to understand the special character of the Jewish people. For Israel was unlike any other nation. Pre-Christian Israel was no mere ethnic grouping: it was not a people like Egypt, Phoenicia or Greece, or even Moab or Edom. "Israel" is fundamentally a sacred name,[4] the name of a people established by a very special event: a covenant with God. Israel was the people of the Covenant, the "people of God". In effect, the covenant of Sinai made the Israelite tribes into one people. The book of Exodus 19:3-8 describes the solemn moment when that people came into being:

> And Moses went up to God, and the LORD called to him out of the mountain, saying, "Thus you shall say to the house of Jacob, and tell the people of Israel: You have seen what I did to the Egyptians, and how I bore you on eagles' wings and brought you to myself. Now therefore, if you will obey my voice and keep my covenant, you shall be my own possession among all peoples ... and you shall be to me a kingdom of priests and a holy nation.... So Moses came and called the elders of the people, and set before them all these words which the LORD had commanded him. And all the people answered together and said, "All that the LORD has spoken we will do."

Israel's vocation

Israel's vocation as "people of God" is linked with a specific requirement: this people must be worthy of its vocation. From that moment on Yahweh is the true King of the tribes of Israel (cf. Dt 33:15), who come together around him (cf. Ex 17:15) and are guided continually by God himself (cf Ex 13:12.21;33:14-17; Num 10:45).

It is true that Israel had a national infrastructure in the form of blood relationships among the tribes. But this ethnic basis is transcended by the specific, supernatural and religious entry of God into the very history of the tribes — a presence of God which penetrates even the remotest corners of national, social and individual life. God is, indeed, the God of all peoples (cf. Rom 3:29) since he is the Creator of them all (cf. Acts 17:24), but he is the God in such a special way of the people of Israel (cf. Num 11: 29; 17:6, Dt 27:9), that no other people can glory in him (cf. Rom 9:11; 11:28; Acts 13:17) — to the extent that other peoples are called "no-people" (Dt 32:21).

The subsequent history of Israel will show that this people will never (or almost never) reach the height of its vocation. And God's way of educating it leads him to inflict tremendous punishment to get it to turn back and be saved (cf. Ez 18:30-32). After the happy times of the Davidic monarchy (which experienced ups and downs), Israel becomes in fact the subject of the no-peoples. First the Northern tribes (721 B.C.) fall into the hands of the Assyrians. Later those of the South (586 B.C.) fall to Babylon, with the first great destruction of Jerusalem and of the temple. The destruction of Jerusalem by Nebuchadnezzar in 586 caused one of the greatest humiliations and afflictions ever experienced by any nation.

It was the most severe of punishments, but its purpose was to soften and convert that people's heart: the eschatological oracles of the prophets foretold the future pardon that God would grant and the return of the scattered tribes to their original unity and the reconstruction of Israel as people of God. All will be restored: Covenant, land, temple and kingdom.... This *restoration* will affect all levels but the lower levels are dependent on the higher ones, these latter being true religious values, which God wishes to reinstate.[5]

The messianic prophecies

In the post-exilic period, the interpretation of the ancient messianic prophecies acquires a special importance.

The character and mission of Jesus Christ, the Messiah, cannot be properly understood, theologically and scientifically, unless they are set in the context of the Old Testament development of messianism; nor can this be understood in any way unless one sees its fulfilment in the Messiah Jesus Christ, Son of God. In other words it is the Old Testament that should be interpreted in the light of the New Testament; but the New Testament, at the level of scientific research, also acquires precise dimensions in the light of the Old.[6]

A summary of the messianic prophecies will help us understand the historical and transcendental figure of Jesus. Even a few brief observations on the ideas Judaism in Jesus' own time had of the Messiah will help us understand many of Jesus Christ's attitudes towards his contemporaries[7] and therefore towards later generations.

The *titulus* on Jesus' cross will be seen to be a sharp reminder, a warning for all future generations, about how the true messianism of Jesus is to be understood; and therefore it will point to the true mission of the Church as the universal instrument it is of the divine salvation[8] brought about *in Jesus*.

Jewish ideas regarding the Messiah

We now come to a complicated question which cannot be dealt with in any systematic way. The idea which Jews of Jesus' time had formed of the Messiah and of the Messianic Kingdom was not one and uniform; it was varied, pluralist. It is fair to say that every large Jewish group had its own idea of the Messiah: the Pharisees one, the Essenes another, certain authors of apocryphal books of relevation another, certain nationalist extremists another. ... [9] This same pluralism is to be found in later Judaism, right down to our own time.

Difficulty arises in the field of methodology: where can we go to discover the most objective, the true common denominator in Jewish thought at the time of Jesus? The answer is complicated: the apocryphal books reflect the particular characteristics of the environment in which each was written; the Qumran documents are very rich but they are also obscure and limited in their scope, since they speak for a small sector of Israel. ... We must come to the conclusion that there was no one prevalent idea of the Messiah and his Kingdom among the Jews of Jesus' time: there was a whole series of ideas, from the concept of the Messiah as the great politico-military leader, heir to the military skills of David, who would conquer all the nations of the world by force of arms, to the idea held by not a few upright and pious Israelites like Simeon, Zachary, the Baptist ... , [10] for whom the Messiah will be the *light of the nations*, the 'lamb of God who takes away the sins of the world'; and consequently the messianic kingdom will be essentially the *forgiveness of sins, the plebs perfecta,* the perfect people. Between these two poles there is a complicated range of views. Innumerable rabbinical writings also present a series of attitudes; however, we can say that for the rabbis the

Messiah and his Kingdom have mainly spiritual characteristics.[11]

As I have said, I do not plan to go into any detail on this subject; but before formulating any conclusion, it is necessary first to outline the development of divine revelation regarding the Messiah and his work, beginning with the authentic source of that revelation, the canonical books of the Old Testament. Jesus Christ, the last revelation of God, "will fulfil" and illuminate the ancient prophecies.

Revelation concerning the Messiah and his work in the setting of Old Testament messianism

From the end of the last century up to our own days rationalist criticism of the origin and development of divine revelation concerning messianism has produced all sorts of conflicting hypotheses. Each new one denies not only the conclusions of the one that went before but even its exegetical and historical-critical principles. They vary from those of Wellhausian inspiration which claim that the whole idea of Messiah evolved slowly and naturally from early very rudimentary notions,[12] to less radical theories of the Sellin School.[13] I don't propose here to get involved in controversies of this type.[14] What I want to do is to take the most brief, simple and sure view possible of Old Testament revelation regarding the future role of the Messiah as God's instrument in bringing salvation.

The figure of a *Messiah* and the idea of *messianism* appear in the Old Testament as integral elements of Israel's and mankind's need of salvation. In this perspective, what the angel says to St Joseph sums up the role of the Messiah very well: "what is conceived in her [Mary] is of the Holy Spirit; she will bear a son, and you shall call his name Jesus, for he will save his people from their sins" (Mt 1:20-21). This *theologoumenon* encapsulates all the main features of the Messiah: the special way he is taken over by the Holy Spirit; his special role as Saviour, freeing the people from the slavery of sin; the salvific consequences of liberation from sin which is the cause of all mankind's misfortunes.

The Promise and the Covenant

In effect, according to Old Testament revelation — followed by the New Testament and particularly explained in the writings of St Paul — God, from the beginning, immediately after the first sin, offered man salvation from the complete mess he had gotten himself into.

At the beginning this salvation of man by God took the form of a PROMISE (Gen 3:15). It became gradually more explicit as biblical history developed — Abraham and the patriarchs, Moses and Sinai; the prophets; Jesus Christ.

God chooses Israel (cf. Ex 10) and makes it his people. He offers it and makes with it an ALLIANCE, a Covenant (cf. Ex 24:3-8) through which he commits himself, in a special way, to the salvation of his people Israel and, by extension, of all mankind, The Alliance, the Covenant, is, then, the method of salvation which God proposes for establishing a relationship with man. All the institutions of the chosen people are subordinate to it and find in it their purpose and meaning.

The theocratic monarchy

Among these institutions one acquires special importance — the Israelite *monarchy* which emerges when the people ask Samuel for a king as the other nations have (cf. 1 Sam 8:5-20). Through the king God addresses the people. Therefore, the King of Israel is regarded as God's representative and lieutenant.

Once established, the Israelite monarchy is the bearer of the Covenant and becomes in fact a further stage in the realisation of Israel's dreams.[15] In this context God makes certain promises to David, which are recorded in 2 Sam 7: 4-16.

> But the same night the word of the LORD came to Nathan, "Go and tell my servant David, 'Thus says the LORD: . . .
>
> I took you from the pasture, from following the sheep, that you should be prince over my people Israel. . . .
>
> When your days are fulfilled and you lie down with your fathers, I will raise up your offspring after you, who shall come forth from your body, and I will establish his kingdom. He shall build a house for my

name, and I will establish the throne of his kingdom for ever. I will be his father, and he shall be my son .... I will not take my steadfast love from him, as I took it from Saul.... And your house and your kingdom shall be made sure for ever before me; your throne shall be established for ever'".

The monarchy, the upholder of the Covenant, acquires in this way a dynastic messianic character: the liberating Messiah will be descended from David, "Son of David". Cf. Gen 49:8-12; Num 23:7-10 and 18-24; 24:3-9 and 15-19 and the many gospel texts which describe the Messiah as the "Son of David".[16]

The prophets

The *prophets*, faithful to their mission, will keep the messianic promises alive, reminding the people of the Covenant and identifying the kings as faithful or unfaithful, depending on whether they have responded to their saving mission: this point of view is the basis of the criticism expressed by the writer of the *Books of the Kings*. Similarly the Psalms show how alive this awareness was of the promises of salvation offered by God through the Davidic monarchy: cf. especially Ps 2; 110; 72; and 138.

It is only when the people has lost hope in human mediation — due to the shortcomings of the kings — that the prophets stress the exclusively divine character of salvation: it is God himself, Yahweh-King, who saves. This gives rise to a current of thought which has become quite strong in contemporary Judaism — *messianism without a Messiah*: important in this connection are texts in the first part of Isaiah: especially Is 1:24 and 10:24.

But this first part of Isaiah is in fact multi-faceted and very rich. Alongside the texts about direct divine salvation, with no mention of any human mediator, we are offered glimpses of a messiah endowed with kingly but also transcendental, supernatural qualities: Cf. especially the series of Immanuel prophecies: Is 7:14; 9:1-6; 11:1-9.

Is 7:14: "Therefore, the Lord himself will give you a

sign. Behold, a young woman shall conceive and bear a son, and shall call his name Immanu-El" (= God is with us).

Is 9:2-6: "The people who walked in darkness have seen a great light.... For to us a child is born, to us a son is given, and the government will be upon his shoulder, and his name will be called 'wonderful counsellor, mighty God, everlasting Father, Prince of peace'. Of the increase of his government and of peace there will be no end, upon the throne of David, and over his kingdom, to establish it, and to uphold it with justice and with righteousness from this time forth and for evermore. The zeal of the Lord of hosts will do this."

For its part, prophetic revelation through Jeremiah and Ezechiel "interiorise" the practice of the mosaic Law (that is, those obligations deriving from the covenant on Sinai) and project messianic hopes onto the future *New Covenant*, the New Testament which Yahweh will make: cf. especially Jer 31:31-35 and Ez 36. We should stress here the great importance of this kind of interiorisation of the messianic idea effected by the prophets.

Is 31:31-33: "Behold, the days are coming, says the Lord, when I will make a new covenant with the house of Israel and the house of Judah.... This is the covenant which I will make with the house of Israel.... I will put my law within them, and I will write it on their hearts; and I will be their God, and they shall be my people."

Meanwhile, the Jewish people were undergoing serious crises — in the north falling to the Assyrians (Samaria fell in 721 B.C.) and in the south succumbing to Nebuchadnezzar (Jerusalem was conquered in 587 B.C.) followed by the great deportation to Babylon. During all these upheavals the prophets correct the over-earthly salvific hopes which the Israelites had woven for themselves: here we would stress the tendency towards *eschatological messianism*. The prophets shed light on this hope of salvation by showing a Saviour Messiah with previously unheard-of characteristics: the Messiah in the person of the suffering Servant of Yah-

16

weh in the second part of Isaiah and in Psalm 21:[17] cf. Is 42: 1-4; 49:1-6; 50:4-9; 52:13-53:12.

He was despised and rejected by men;
   a man of sorrows, and acquainted with grief;
and as one from whom men hide their faces
   he was despised, and we esteemed him not.

Surely he has borne our griefs and carried our sorrows;
yet we esteemed him stricken, smitten by God, and
   afflicted.
But he was wounded for our transgressions,
   he was bruised for our iniquities;
upon him was the chastisement that made us whole,
   and with his stripes we are healed.
All we like sheep have gone astray;
   we have turned every one to his own way;
and the LORD has laid on him the iniquity of us all.

He was oppressed, and he was afflicted,
   yet he opened not his mouth;
like a lamb that is led to the slaughter,
   and like a sheep that before its shearers is dumb,
   so he opened not his mouth.
By oppression and [false] judgment he was taken
   away . . .
   he was cut off out of the land of the living,
   stricken for the transgression of my people. . .
Yet it was the will of the LORD to bruise him;
   he has put him to grief;
when he makes himself an offering for sin,
   he shall see his offspring, he shall prolong his days;
the will of the LORD shall prosper in his hand;
   he shall see the fruit of the travail of his soul and be
      satisfied;
by his knowledge shall the righteous one, my servant,
   make many to be accounted righteous;
   and he shall bear their iniquities.
Therefore I will divide him a portion with the great,
   and he shall divide the spoil with the strong;
because he poured out his soul to death,
   and was numbered with the transgressors;
   yet he bore the sin of many,

and made intercession for the
     transgressors.

Finally the eschatological horizon is lit up by the figure
of an earthly — but — transcendental Messiah: Daniel 17:
14ff presents the figure of the "Son of man", mysterious-
ly transcendent, and this will be the title most used by
Jesus Christ. The short book of the prophet Micah in some
way gives a synthesis of the whole range of messianic in-
sights.

Yahweh's Anointed

As far as the terminology used in connection with the concept of Messiah[18] is concerned, in Samuel's time the parti-
ciple *masiaj, anointed,* is used to designate Saul and David:
it was by anointing that they were constituted kings of
Israel.[19] However, it cannot be said that the title of *masiaj*
was used at that time exclusively to designate kings of
Israel: the same word is used to describe the calling of the
priest who also undergoes the rite of anointing.[20]

In the later centuries of the monarchy the expression
"Anointed of God" is the standard one used to refer to the
king — the reason being the divine character of Israelite roy-
alty and the idea that in the last analysis the true king of
Israel is Yahweh himself, who chooses the king-anointed as
his representative or lieutenant on earth. Alongside this
dominant or primary use of the title of Messiah to refer to
the king of Israel, the same word continues to be used to
refer to others who have received a mission from God which
is distinct from the king's. For example, Eliseus has to be
"anointed as prophet"[21] and, later on, even a foreign king,
Cyrus the Persian, will also be called "anointed, masiaj".[22]

Conclusions regarding the Messiah and his work in the messianic texts of the Old Testament

The central idea of hope in a messiah in the Old Testament is that Yahweh will intervene in an extraordinary and definitive way to save the chosen people and reveal himself as absolute lord of all mankind and of the cosmos. In other words, the kingdom of God will be restored in a spectacular and perfect way.

The establishment of the kingdom of God, however, even though it is the result of Yahweh's omnipotence, is still attributed in the most important texts of the prophetic books and in not a few of the psalms, to a rather ill-defined personality — *the anointed of Yahweh, the Messiah*; these texts indicate that it will be the Messiah directly who establishes the kingdom of God. The work of the Messiah, despite the varied ways it is presented by the prophets, has certain characteristics common to most of them: he will be the new and definitive restorer, the convenor of the people in their future and definitive history, which will be filled with all the treasures of the messianic peace; the Messiah will re-unite the *scattered members* of the chosen people; he will make Yahweh's new covenant with his people; he will reign with unique authority, power, wisdom and justice (= holiness) and will be God's instrument for the conversion of all the nations, allowing them to share in the messianic salvation granted to Israel.

The Messiah will be the instrument of the salvation and liberation of the future people, over which he will reign *for ever*. He is depicted as a new and perfect Moses, a liberator, leader, saviour, teacher and lawgiver of the future and definitive people of the new Covenant, even to the point of transcending the merely human condition. The notions of Messiah and of the ideal, future, new Israel always go hand in hand, the one implying the other.

This future new people of God acquires a universal character through its taking into itself all the nations of the world, so as to constitute a single holy peaceful and prosperous people under the everlasting benevolent rule of the Messiah.

The figure of the Messiah and his work in the Judaism of Jesus' time: apocryphal literature

Documents exist to prove that there was widespread and intense expectation of the Messiah in the Judeo-Palestinian world during the time when the Incarnate Word was born and lived on earth. We have not the references to it in the New Testament, but what is particularly interesting is the testimony of the various Jewish apocryphal writings of the period around Jesus' lifetime.[23]

In the apocryphal book of *Henoch* (*Parables*, chaps 37, 69, 71) the Messiah is called *the Chosen One, God's Anointed* and *Son of man*.[24]

In the *Testament of the Twelve Patriarchs* he is represented as the king who is to come out of Judah (there is also a text which speaks of a Messiah descended from Levi).

In the *Odes* or *Apocryphal Psalms of Solomon* the Messiah is given all sorts of titles: *Son of David, King of Israel* or *King of the Jews, the Lord's Anointed*. He appears both as a heavenly being and as a man, for on the one hand the transcendental character of the Messiah as closely united to God is stressed; and on the other his human condition is clearly expressed. Taken as a whole, the Messiah emerges as endowed with great spiritual qualities — but, due to his descent from David, he is more a human figure, with a strong temporalist meaning.[25]

The seventeenth Psalm of Solomon

Let us take for example the seventeenth Psalm of Solomon, which critics date around the middle of the first century before Christ. This apocryphal psalm outlines the sort of idea of the Messiah held by many pious Jews of the time. It can be summed up as follows: The Messiah is King, descended from David (son of David); he has been raised up directly by God to free Israel from its enemies; he will be invested with power from on high (divine power) and will be endowed with singular wisdom and knowledge; he will gather together all the scattered tribes of the people; he will avenge the chosen people on its oppressors; he will reign gloriously and will shepherd the people of God in justice. We can conclude that, not withstanding the high conception implied by this Messiah, there are many signs of a messianic nationalism which fails to break out of the limitations of an earth-bound outlook and of patriotic anguish.[26]

Psalm XVII:

23 Behold, O Lord, and raise up unto them
    their king, the son of David, at the time in the
    which thou seest, O God, that he may reign over
    Israel thy servant.

24 And gird him with strength, that he may shatter
    unrighteous rulers.

25 And that he may purge Jerusalem from nations   ·
    that trample (her) down to destruction.

26 Wisely, righteously he shall thrust out sinners
    from (the) inheritance; he shall destroy the pride
    of the sinners as a potter's vessel . . .

27 He shall destroy the godless nations with the word
    of his mouth; at his rebuke nations shall flee before
    him, and he shall reprove sinners for the thoughts
    of their heart.

28 And he shall gather together a holy people, whom
    he shall lead in righteousness, and he shall judge
    the tribes of the people that has been sanctified
    by the Lord his God.

29 And he shall not suffer unrighteousness to lodge
    any more in their midst, nor shall there dwell with
    them any man that knoweth wickedness.

30　For he shall know them, that they are all sons of
　　their God. And he shall divide them according to
　　their tribes upon the land.

31　And neither sojourner nor alien shall sojourn with
　　them any more. He shall judge peoples and nations
　　in the wisdom of his righteousness.

32　And he shall have the heathen nations to serve
　　him under his yoke; and he shall glorify the Lord
　　in a place to be seen of (?) all the earth.

33　And he shall purge Jerusalem making it holy as
　　of old.

34　So that nations shall come from the ends of the
　　earth to see his glory, bringing as gifts her sons
　　who had fainted,

35　and to see the glory of the Lord, wherewith God
　　hath glorified her.

36.　And he shall be a righteous king, taught of God,
　　over them, and there shall be no unrighteousness
　　in his days in their midst, for all shall be holy and
　　their king the anointed of the Lord.

37　For he shall not put his trust in horse and rider
　　and bow, nor shall he multiply for himself gold
　　and silver for war, nor shall he gather confidence
　　from (?) a multitude (?) for the day of battle.

38　The Lord himself is his king, the hope of him that
　　is mighty through his hope in God. All nations
　　shall be in fear before him.

39　For he will smite the earth with the word of his
　　mouth for ever.

40　He will bless the people of the Lord with wisdom
　　and gladness.

41　And he himself (will be) pure from sin, so that he

may rule a great people. He will rebuke rulers, and remove sinners by the might of his word.

42 And (relying) upon his God, throughout his days, he will not stumble; for God will make him mighty by means of (his) holy spirit. And wise by means of the spirit of understanding, with strength and righteousness.

43 And the blessing of the Lord will be with him: he will be strong and stumble not.

44 His hope will be in the Lord: who then can prevail against him? He will be mighty in his works, and strong in the fear of God.

45 (He will be) shepherding the flock of the Lord faithfully and righteously, and will suffer none among them to stumble in their pasture.

46 He will lead them all aright, and there will be no pride among them that any among them should be oppressed.

47 This (will be) the majesty of the king of Israel whom God knoweth; he will raise him up over the house of Israel to correct him.

48 His words (shall be) more refined than costly gold, the choicest in the assemblies he will judge the peoples, the tribes of the sanctified.

49 His words (shall be) like the words of the holy ones in the midst of sanctified peoples.

50 Blessed be they that shall be in those days, in that they shall see the good fortune of Israel which God shall bring to pass in the gathering together of the tribes.

51 May the Lord hasten his mercy upon Israel! May he deliver us from the uncleanness of unholy

enemies! The Lord himself is our king for ever
and ever.

These ideas about the Messiah which we find in the
seventeenth Psalm of Solomon are repeated in one form or
another in other poems in the same collection (for example
Psalm 18).

A nationalist Messiah

Obviously this conception of the Messiah and his kingdom
is in contrast with what we have seen outlined in the sacred,
canonical books of the Old Testament — for example the
second part of Isaiah, Zechariah; the canonical Psalm 21, etc.
And yet the apocryphal psalms of Solomon are set in the
more spiritual line of Jewish writings of the period. It would
seem that the Jews of the time, even in the most pious sec-
tors, found it impossible, perhaps due to their difficult
political circumstances, to rise clearly above aspirations to
political independence.[27]

Within these messianic conceptions, which always tend
to be polarised towards nationalism, there is no room for
any notion of a suffering, humiliated Messiah. This meant
that the prophecies in the poem of the Servant of Yahweh
(Isaiah chaps 42-53), in Psalm 21, etc., were applied, in
Jewish exegesis at Jesus' time, to personalities other than
the Messiah. The fashionable interpretation had a strong
influence even on Jesus' twelve apostles prior to his resurrection and even in the first days after the resurrection:

"We had hoped that he was the one to redeem Israel.
Yes, and besides all this, it is now three days since this
happened" (Lk 24:21).

So when they had come together, they asked him,
"Lord, will you at this time restore the kingdom to
Israel?" (Acts 1:6).

The apocryphal literature

If we look at all the apocryphal literature between the two

testaments (*The Book of Jubilees, The Assumption of Moses* and the *Apocalypse of Moses*) or the other Jewish writings (Flavius Josephus, Qumrân, the oldest surviving traces of rabbinical literature) we find, with various nuances, the same nationalistic tendency in messianic outlook as obtained in Jesus' time.

We can conclude that, during this period, practically all the Jews had the feeling that the ancient solemn promises made by God in favour of the people of Israel were about to be fulfilled. God had fixed his day, his time, for intervening in a spectacular way, even more dramatically than he had done at the time of liberation from Egypt. And around Jesus' time, precisely because of their dire straits, the Jews had an interior presentiment that when they least expected, soon, their salvation would appear. Apocryphal literature fuelled their hopes and in ever more varied circles the solemn notes were struck: liberation must come and soon, in a spectacular way: the Kingdom of David would be restored, the nation freed from foreign subjection, its frontiers expanded further than ever before, the pagans conquered by the King-Messiah and subjected to the religion of the true God; Jerusalem would become the centre of the universe, from whose four quarters the scattered remnants of Israel would gather and the pagan nations would also come to render worship to Yahweh.[29]

Alongside the noblest of spiritual aspirations there arise visions of the national rehabilitation and material prosperity that will mark the Messianic age: the land of Israel will enjoy wonderful fertility; water, fields, trees and flocks will abound.

All these ideas are in the air at the time when Jesus is revealing that he is the Messiah. Jesus will be seen to be very careful to prevent his countrymen following him as an earthly Messiah-King. His prudence in manifesting the fact that he is the Messiah can be seen in the Gospels, perhaps particularly in St Mark's. Modern criticism has termed it the 'messianic secret'.

Nor should we forget that the Jewish ruling classes had a completely closed attitude to the religious teaching and behaviour of Jesus. Why did official Judaism not accept Jesus? This is a great mystery; it has been the subject of many studies, beginning perhaps with St Justin Martyr's *Dialogue with Triphon* (second century) and it is still being explored from all kinds of angles. We cannot discuss it here, because it is outside the scope of this lecture.

Jewish nationalism in Jesus' time

The messianic notions of Jews in Jesus' time gave rise to various movements and groupings of activists. These transferred to the political sphere the religious interpretations we have been reviewing — debasing them in the process. Thus, alongside the more important religious groups — Pharisees, Saduccees, Essenes of Qumrân etc. — you can find a variety of attitudes to the political scene in Palestine: Zealots, Sicarii, Herodians, etc.[31]

Aspirations to independence

We should remember that the Jewish nation had lost its independence some sixty years before the birth of Jesus. The Herodian monarchy, despite its comfortable economic circumstances, failed to satisfy the Jewish people's aspirations to independence. The replacement of the Herodian regime by direct government through Roman procurators further wounded national pride. From the year 6 A.D., when Judea became a Roman procuratorial Province, depending from the legate in Syria, to the year 70 when Jerusalem was destroyed by Titus, Jewish nationalistic feeling against Rome became more and more pronounced.

It is true that Rome tried to leave a certain internal autonomy to the countries it took over. In fact the Jewish nation enjoyed more autonomy than others: the country's senate, the Sanhedrin, had charge of ordinary civil and religious affairs, under the watchful eye of the Procurator, who was particularly concerned with public order, with the *total* of tax revenue, and with the province's external relations.[32]

But this type of political status was merely tolerated by the Jews; it was in conflict with the theocratic idea which had been a feature of the state ever since Israel became a nation.

The Gospels themselves give us interesting historical information on this situation. For example they show us how at the time of Jesus' public ministry (c. 30 A.D.) anyone who had a position which meant collaboration with the Romans was looked down on: this was the case with publicans or tax collectors.

The "Resistance": the Zealots

The Jews' instinctive aversion to being ruled by Gentiles — in this case the Roman empire — took on forms of religious-political resistance. We know about the *Zealot* movement (from the Greek zêlos = zeal). The Zealots were in fact committed to fighting for national independence, to open the way for the restoration of the Davidic government which in turn would herald the Messianic kingdom.

Recent studies[33] distinguish the Zealots properly so called, who formed a broad politico-religious nationalist party, already extremist in character, from other minority activist groups which were even more extreme — such as the *Sicarii* — who had been given this name by the Romans because they wore a *sica* (Latin) or short dagger under their clothes.[34] These *Sicarii* supported violence as being the only effective way to achieve national independence and open the way for the Messianic kingdom.

So, we can say that, during the years of Jesus' public ministry, resistance to the Roman occupation was *the* basic Jewish question; and that, due to special character of Palestinian Judaism, this question was both religious and political. The Roman authorities, in turn, became more and more obsessed with this nationalist question and saw "zealotism" lurking everywhere.[35] The situation, became steadily worse until some thirty years after Jesus' death it erupted in the form of the first Jewish war, culminating in the terrible destruction of Jerusalem in the year 70.

It was in the context of this religio-political nationalistic ferment that Jesus' public ministry took place. We should bear this context in mind if we want to try to evaluate accurately the reason for Jesus' discretion in gradually making known that he was the Messiah.

Going beyond political messianism, seen in Jesus' choice of his disciples

In a deeply symbolic way, Jesus convened the new people of God, his Church, by first calling twelve Israelites who, in both parallel and contrast with the twelve Hebrew patriarchs, were to be the pillars of this new line which would derive not from human but from spiritual generation. But he called them in the concrete context of the Jewish nation which we have been examining.

Among these twelve followers were men drawn from all the prevailing tendencies in political and temporal questions.

The "political affiliation" of the Apostles

First, Simon Bariôna, called Peter. Who was he? A Galilean fisherman, yes; yet even at the last supper and at Gethsemani he carried a sword tucked under his ample outer garment, and he was quick to use it when Jesus was arrested. Peter does not conceive that Jesus, whom he recognises and loves as the Messiah, should undergo suffering. Some modern critics, on analysing philologically Simon's first surname (that is, *Bariôna,* used in Matthew 16:17), claim that it is not correct to call him "son of Jonah". Iôna would have nothing to do with *John*, or with Jonas, but would be a word of Acadian origin — perhaps imported during the Assyrian occupation of Samaria and Galilee — which means "terror". Thus, if the theory is correct, Bar-Iôna should be translated as "Son of terror" that is to say, "terrorist".[36] However, it seams clear, from recent philological studies, that Iona is the popular Galilaic pronunciation of *Iohanna,* that is, John. But it is difficult to explain why Peter should be carrying a sword, an outmoded practice in civil society at the time, whether Roman or Jewish.

There is certainly no doubt about the other Simon being associated with the Zealots. In Lk 6:15 he is mentioned as "Simon, who was called the Zealot, *zêlôtês*". In Acts 1:13 he is simply "Simon the Zealot". It is quite definite that *zêlôtês* designates specifically and exclusively the supporters of the Zealot nationalistic group. For their part, Mt 10:4 and Mk 3:18 call this Simon *"ho kananaios"*, which is the Greek transcription (not the translation of the original Aramaic noun which means precisely *Zêlôtês*.[37] Even though they sound similar, *kananaios* has nothing to do with *Kanaan*, the ancient name of pre-Hebrew Palestine; when in English this is transcribed as "the Cananean" it cannot be taken as a name relating to a tribe or as a patronymic.

Nowadays there is a certain acceptance among scholars of the word *Iscariot* meaning *sicarius*, assassin, largely for two philological reasons: (1) the old idea that *"Iskarioth"* meant "man from Karioth" has no basis: there is no sign of Karioth referring to any place — town, site, mountain, river, etc. — whereas it is easily recognisable as a popular Greek transcription of *sicarius*. Therefore it must be a nickname deriving from Judas' previous connection with this most extreme and violent Jewish nationalistic group.[38]

Facing these three apostles who were aligned with the nationalistic current, more or less extremist, we have another, author of the first gospel, the "tax collector", or publican (*ho telones*) Matthew (Mt 10:4; Mk 3:18; Lk 6:15; Acts 1:13): this apostle and evangelist, clearly a publican by profession (cf. Mt 9:9-13; Mk 1:14-17; Lk 5:27-32), was therefore regarded as a "collaborator" with the established political regime. Yet, he became a member of the group of the twelve disciples who will follow Jesus.

We do not have information about the other apostles which would indicate definitely or possibly that they held any particular attitude to public affairs. We only know that James and John, whom Jesus called "sons of Thunder" showed a certain xenophobia towards the Samaritans; and they "were acquaintances of the High Priest" Caiphas, which allowed them enter his palace when Jesus was being questioned and obtain entry for Peter also.

Jesus chose certain specific men to found his Church.

This mission transcended their political affiliation, profession and social condition. Following Jesus gradually led them to uproot their previous merely human outlook. Patiently and gradually, Jesus opened up for them new perspectives, which were immensely more profound and religious. The light of the events of Paschaltide, the words of the Risen Jesus at his appearances and the special grace of the Holy Spirit after Pentecost were to turn these men into the true Apostles of Jesus — all but one, Judas, who failed to shed his selfish human outlook.

The divine character of Jesus' messiahship: exegesis of certain Gospel texts

We have briefly surveyed the situation of Palestinian Judaism and its nationalistic outlook at the time the Messiah began his public ministry. We move now to examine Jesus' persistent attitude to the religio-political situation and to the messianic expectation of his time. We might anticipate ourselves by saying that Jesus' faithfulness to his special salvific mission, the most intimate communion of Jesus' humanity with God by means of the hypostatic union of human nature with the second Person of the Trinity, would lead us to expect, in advance, that Jesus Christ would transcend each and every Jewish religious group.

Exegesis of the evangelical texts very clearly bears this out: to understand Jesus, to believe in him, first as Messiah and then as Son of God, every Israelite of his time had to shed any temporalist attitude, any idea of a nationalist messianism.[39]

Jesus is tempted in the desert: Satan's first attempt to "temporalise" Jesus' divine mission.

The concept of temptation ($\pi\epsilon\iota\rho\alpha\sigma\mu\acute{o}\varsigma$, *massâh*) in the Bible is, to say the least, ambivalent: sometimes it means *test*, sometimes *seduction*.[40] The subject of the verb *tempt* ($\pi\epsilon\iota\rho\acute{a}\zeta\epsilon\iota\nu$, *nissâh*), when the context is religious, is ultimately either God or the Devil. It can also be man, but only in so far as he is moved to tempt another by divine or demoniacal influence. In gist — though this may be simplifying it too much — when God "tempts" it means that God "is testing" a person's quality — his fidelity, his fortitude in resisting the attraction of vice, his true motivation, etc. When it is the devil who is the tempter he is "trying to seduce", to deceive, to make man sin, to lead him astray.

In the history of salvation temptation, in its dual meaning, occupies an important place and occurs frequently at key stages in the history of the people of God. All the main personalities in sacred history are "tempted": Adam and Eve, Abraham, Moses ..., the entire people during its pilgrimage in the desert. The three Synoptic Gospels all show Jesus being led by the Spirit into the desert (Mt 4:1; Mk 1:2; Lk 4:1) and go on to tell how he was "tempted" there by the devil. Matthew stresses that Jesus was led into the desert "to be tempted by the devil" (Mt 4:1). He has a theological didactic purpose in putting it this way: in keeping with the very obvious focus of the First Gospel, the prophecies of the Old Testament "are fulfilled" in Jesus — for the whole of that Testament is a general prophecy about Jesus. That interpretation is quite correct which sees in Jesus' exposure to these temptations a multiple pedagogic purpose on God's part: (1) on the one hand, the temptations of the patriarchs and prophets of the Old Testament and of the people of Israel itself are a pre-figuring of the "temptations" to which Jesus is to be subjected. (2) On the other hand, the "falls" of the people of Israel during the Exodus, its failure to live up to its divine calling, are going to be "rectified" by Jesus' fidelity to his mission. (3) Finally, according to the same Gospel, Jesus' life is an introduction to the subsequent life of the Church. According to this approach, Jesus' victory over the "Tempter" should be the prelude to and exemplar of the subsequent struggles of the Church against "temptations" by the powers of hell.[42]

Mark does not detail these temptations of Jesus, but Matthew and Luke both give us accounts which are concise and profound. Both Evangelists speak of *three temptations*. What I want to stress here, as the common denominator of all three, is that Satan tries to debase Jesus' messianism by getting Jesus to turn it to his personal advantage: he wants him to "temporalise" his transcendental passion: (a) to use his powers to remedy a very temporal situation, by turning stones into bread, at a point when Jesus' hunger, after fasting, must be very acute. (b) He wants to provoke him to vanity and pride by asking God to perform an unnecessary miracle: he wants him rashly to provoke God by throwing himself off the pinnacle of the Temple so as to force God to do a spectacular miracle which would earn Jesus immense prestige but would be a huge temptation for his humility. (c) Finally, he offers him dominion over all the kingdoms of the world.[43]

This third temptation in Matthew (the second in Luke) is the most typically pseudo-messianic: Jesus would become the earthly messianic King. His energetic reply "Ὕπαγε, Σατανᾶ (Mt 4:10), Begone, Satan" is similar to the reply he made later to Peter: "Ὕπαγε ὀπίσω μου Σατανᾶ, when at the first announcement of his passion Peter tries to persuade Jesus that he should not even think of that event occurring (Mt 16: 21-23; Mk 8: 31-33; Lk 9:22). The energy with which Jesus rejects this temporalist messianism (which would reduce his transcendental mission to a matter of earthly, political power) is, at it were, a reparation for or a rectification of the infidelities of the people of Israel from the Exodus onwards.[44] But by the same token it is a norm, a vivid warning given by Jesus to the true Israel of God, the Church, in order to establish it firmly in the transcendence of its divine salvific mission without any reduction of that mission to the temporal sphere, in the face of the successive satanic temptations which it will be subjected to in the course of the centuries.

The "temptations" of Jesus in the desert have both the dimensions we indicated: they were a divine "test" of his fidelity: "he was led by the Spirit into the desert" (Mt 4:1; Mk 1:12; Lk 4:1) and they are also an "attempt at seduction" by the devil. These "temptations" of Jesus were not the only ones, as we shall see: they occurred again and again during his life. Similarly, "temptation" as a divine "test" and a satanic "attempt at seduction" are features of the history and of the future of the people of God until the end of time. The Church must be aware that these twin difficulties have been faced in the past and must be faced continually until the end of time. And let us spell it out, all the "temptations" the Church experiences and will experience have a common denominator just as Jesus' temptations had — fidelity to the divine supra-temporal transcendence of its salvific mission.

The Scribes and Pharisees ask Jesus for a miraculous sign which will prove he is the Messiah.

Mt 12: 38-40:

38   Then some of the Scribes and Pharisees said to him, "Teacher, we wish to see a sign from you"(σημεῖον).

39   But he answered them, "An evil and adulterous generation seeks for a sign; but no sign shall be given it except the sign of the prophet Jonah.

40   "For, as Jonah was three days and three nights in the belly of the whale, so will the Son of man be three days and three nights in the heart of the earth . . . "

(parallel texts: Mt 16:1-4; Mk 8:11-12; Lk 11:29-30).

The context of this passage in the Gospel of Matthew indicates that this kind of request for a prodigious sign (σημεῖον) implied, on the part of the Scribes and Pharisees, the rejection of the probative value of the series of miracles or "works of the Messiah" which Jesus performed and which the Evangelist has grouped together in chapters 8 and 9.

The Scribes' and Pharisees' call for a sign was not aimed, in good will, at "believing" in him; their intention was hypocritical: they wanted to "tempt" him: this can be clearly seen from the parallel account in Mk 8:11-12 and Lk 11:16. Essentially their call for a miracle is the same sort of "temptation" as those in the desert. I do not think it is unsound to see in Jesus' reply, so fulminating, so harsh, the same attitude as he has in the desert: basically here once again is the flattering, devious, satanic temptation, now on the lips of those men. Once again he is asked for a spectacular miracle. But no: the only sign they will get will be the one already planned — the death and resurrection of Jesus, prefigured in the Jonah episode. Even the adjective he applies to his questioners — *evil, malicious,* πονηρός , refers in the language of Jesus and the New Testament to the evil one, that is to say, the Devil. This explains the harshness of his thundering reply.

Once again, Jesus refuses to bend, in any way at all, to reduce his messianism to the level of the nationalistic ideal or of the spectacle which those scribes and Pharisees propose to him.

The division of the inheritance

Lk 12:13-14

13 One of the multitude said to him, "Teacher, bid my brother divide the inheritance with me".

14 But he said to him, "Man, who made me a judge or divider over you?"

The scene is so clear, and it is narrated with such simplicity and freshness. The man in question is interested in his own particular financial problems: he has not grasped in any way the spiritual transcendence of what Jesus is offering him. He sees in Jesus only a rabbi of great authority and personality, who can influence his stubborn brother, perhaps the oldest in the family, who may have over applied (to his own benefit) the prescriptions of Deuteronomy 21:17 regarding inheritance division.[45] The petitioner is perhaps a good example of that common tendency of approaching moral, hierarchical or religious authorities not in order to seek guidance for one's spiritual life but just to solve material problems.

But what interests us now is Jesus' attitude which comes through in this little encounter which St Luke, under the influence of the Holy Spirit, has preserved for us: Jesus, resolutely, leaves no room for doubt; he immediately rejects the request: this cannot be a sign that he is insensitive towards some possible family injustice — or even social injustice — but because intervention in such matters he considers to be óutside the mission he has received from his Father. By this attitude Jesus shows that he has not been sent to regulate and solve directly the infinite number of material and legal matters — even matters to do with justice — which we humans get involved in from the very moment we get a sense of ownership. All these endless problems should be solved by ourselves and by our own family, social and political authorities in the course of human history. However, Jesus himself — it is enough to recall the sermon on the Mount — claims the title of Teacher who has come to give the moral criterion which should *inform* the just action of men and women in matters of this kind.[46]

How prosaic Christ's role as Saviour and revealer would be if it were reduced to solving one by one every injustice that arises among men! The question of the inheritance would be solved — automatically — if both brothers had taken to heart the spiritual teaching of Christ. Then, they themselves would have arrived at a brotherly and just accord, without needing to implicate the Son of God in people's petty disputes and in temporal legal options which the mere passage of time and changes of circumstances would alter.[47]

First announcement of the Passion

Mt 16:21-23 (par. texts Mk 8:31-33; Lk 9:22).

> From that time Jesus began to show his disciples that he must go to Jerusalem and suffer many things from the elders and chief priests and scribes, and be killed, and on the third day be raised. And Peter took him and began to rebuke him, saying, "God forbid, Lord! This shall never happen to you." But he turned and said to Peter, "Get behind me, Satan!($"T\pi\alpha\gamma\epsilon\ \dot{o}\pi\dot{\iota}\sigma\omega$ μov, $\Sigma\alpha\tau\alpha\nu\bar{\alpha}$); You are a hindrance to me; for you are not on the side of God, but of men."

We must remember that the Evangelist places this account immediately after that of the confession at Caesarea Philippi, where Jesus has just received from his disciples, and particularly from Peter, the first explicit confession of faith in himself as Messiah. Just before this, in Caesarea, in response to Peter's confession "You are the Christ, the Son of the living God ($\Sigma\acute{v}\ \epsilon\bar{\iota}\ \dot{o}\ X\rho\iota\sigma\tau\acute{o}\varsigma\ \dot{o}\ \Upsilon\iota\acute{o}\varsigma\ \tau o\bar{v}$ $\vartheta\epsilon o\bar{v}\ \tau o\bar{v}\ Z\bar{\omega}\nu\tau o\varsigma$) " (Mt 16:16), Jesus obviously full of joy, replies, "Blessed are you, Simon Bariôna. For flesh and blood has not revealed this to you, but my Father who is in heaven" (Mt 16:17).

It should be stressed that what fills Jesus with joy in Caesarea is the fact that Peter acknowledges his transcendental messianism: this acknowledgement comes not from men or from Satan but from his heavenly Father.[48] But because Jesus knows how weak human beings are and realises that Peter, like his other disciples, will be sifted by Satan (cf. Lk 22:31-32) he wants to warn and purify the minds and hearts of the Twelve so that they will not be deceived by the Tempter. Therefore, following on from Caesarea episode, Jesus tells them quite clearly that he is not the nationalistic Messiah-King which so many Jews are expecting nor the political Messiah which Satan wants, but the humiliated and transcendent Messiah-Son of God, who saves by ways quite distinct from those of men and devils.

In the light of this we can easily understand Jesus' instant and forthright reaction to Peter when Peter wants to dissuade him from embracing divine messianism. Peter and the Apostles, whose successors will be bishops of the Church down to the end of this present world, should be quite clear in their mind about the high, transcendent nature of their mission, which is the extension of that of Jesus. That is why he upbraids Peter so strongly — and in him the Church down the ages: any kind of reduction of his divine mission to a "temporalist" notion must be regarded as — is, in fact — a temptation of the devil: they have a very grave duty to react against it in an absolutely clear way.

Satan will tempt Jesus' disciples

Lk 22-31-34:

31   "Simon, Simon, behold, Satan demanded to have you, that he might sift you like wheat,

32   but I have prayed for you that your faith may not fail; and when you have turned again, strengthen your brethren".

33   And he said to him, "Lord, I am ready to go with you to prison and to death".

34   He said, "I tell you Peter the cock will not crow this day until you three times deny that you know me".

The repetition of the name Simon clearly gives Jesus'

words a solemn character. Due to Peter's denials, which Jesus goes on to foretell (Lk 22:34), the omission of the name *Cephas*, Peter, is fully intended: his cowardice is not going to say much for his rock-like quality. This text is to be found only in Luke — not in Matthew or Mark. But Luke's fidelity to his sources (a fact verified right through his two books) and the foretelling of the weakness of the leader of the Apostles, give Luke's narrative a scholarly guarantee of authenticity (additional to the guarantee stemming from its divine inspiration) such that no serious critic could doubt the historicity of the episode.

The tenour of the passage suggests that there is something here which is similar to the temptations of Jesus in the desert, and in general to the role of "temptation" throughout salvation history. Thus, Simon and the Apostles, like Adam and Eve, Abraham and Moses, and Jesus himself, are going to have their fidelity "tested" by God, and Satan will "attempt to seduce" them. The aorist ἐξῃτήσατο means not only that Satan has asked to be given power to tempt them but that God has in some way granted his request. So, just as Jesus "was led by the Spirit into the desert to be tempted" before beginning his mission, Peter and the Apostles are going to be "tested" and "tempted". Like Adam and Eve, Peter and the Apostles will fall in this "test-temptation", but Jesus has prayed for them and they will recover, all of them will repent, all but Judas.

But, what is the nature of this "test-temptation" which Peter and the Apostles undergo? It has to do precisely with the transcendental, divine character of Jesus' messiahship. To put it another way, what causes them to flee is their disconcertion: Jesus' reaction when he is arrested in the Garden is not that of the Warrior-Messiah: when Christ once again, on this occasion, clearly expresses the transcendental character of his messiahship, his disciples fail to understand; they are disillusioned and disconcerted. Luke 22:31-33 is very nicely situated by the Evangelist — after the last Supper; for the second part of the narrative, that is, the foretelling of Peter's denials, comes exactly in the same place in all four Gospels; indeed, Mark locates it very exactly: "And when they had sung a hymn [the hymns at the last Supper] they went out to the Mount of Olives..." and then goes on to the prophecy of Peter's denials (cf. Mt 26:31-35; Mk 14:26-31; Jn 13:36-38).

We were saying that the "test-temptation" of Peter and the Apostles consisted precisely in recognising the divine character of Jesus messiahship; and in fact only some two or three hours after this Jesus was apprehended in the garden of Olives:

> Then Simon Peter, having a sword, drew it and struck the high priest's slave and cut off his right ear. The slave's name was Malchus. Jesus said to Peter, "Put your sword into its sheath; shall I not drink the cup which my Father has given me? (John 18:10-11; cf. Mt 26:51-56; Mk 14:47-49; Lk 22:47-50).

Peter, as on so many other occasions, had taken the lead among his colleagues, whether in speaking or in acting. A moment of decision had arrived so he used his sword to strike at the head of the first person who dared lay hands on Jesus. The blow partly missed and instead of cutting his head in two he only reached the man's ear. Peter and the Apostles had not yet understood the nature of Jesus' messiahship.[49] They had not yet rid their minds of the idea of a Messiah-King. The Roman cohort did not shock Peter, nor did the High Priest's henchmen. Like a brave man, a loyal friend, an enthusiastic "supporter" of Jesus, he moved to defend him, by killing people and exposing himself to death. Once again, Jesus severely used the situation to show his disciples what his Messiah role in fact was:

> "Put your sword back into its place; for all who take the sword will perish by the sword. Do you think that I cannot appeal to my Father, and he will at once send me more than twelve legions of angels? But how then should the scriptures be fulfilled, that it must be so?" (Mt 26:52-55).

Jesus definitely renounced violence, cured the wounded slave, and gave himself up to the Roman cohort and the officers of the High Priest. The disciples, immensely disillusioned, took fright and fled. They had fallen into the "test-temptation", they had been caught, for a few hours, by the satanic temptation of seeking in Jesus the political Messiah.

Mt 27:39-43 (parallel: Mk 15:29-32; Lk 23:35-43:

> And those who passed by derided him, wagging their heads and saying, "You who would destroy the temple and build it in three days, save yourself! If you are Son of God, come down from the cross." So also the chief priests, with the scribes and elders, mocked him, saying, "He saved others; he cannot save himself. He is the King of Israel; let him come down now from the cross, and we will believe in him. He trusts in God; let God deliver him now, if he desires him; for he said, 'I am the Son of God.'"

Essentially these insults coincide content-wise with the second temptation in the desert according to Matthew (4:5-7) and the third according to Luke (4:9-12): in the desert Satan incites Jesus to throw himself off the pinnacle of the Temple to show that he is Son of God (εἰ υἱός εἶ τοῦ Θεοῦ) without the definite article: "Son" not "the Son"). The very same phrase is used here: (εἰ υἱός εἶ τοῦ Θεοῦ = if you are Son of God.

It is difficult to imagine that on either occasion the tempters realised the exact implications of their expression, Son of God. They must have been referring to a merely human condition, although one of exceptional quality. Thus, the phrase on the lips of these men would mean: if you are the Messiah (in their sense of the word Messiah).

The chief priests, scribes and elders of the people repeat the same accusation-temptation as the other passers-by, but with a more explicit messianic meaning: "if he is the king of Israel, let him come down from the cross and we will believe in him..."

. The phrase "if you are Son of God" — used by Satan in the desert and by some of the Jews at the Crucifixion — makes it difficult not to think that it is ultimately Satan who utters it in both cases — directly in the desert and indirectly in the second case. The way Matthew puts it seems to suggest this. They are both instances of the same "temptation-incitement" to get Jesus to give an ostentatious sign of his messiahship and at the same time disobey God's will. But Jesus, precisely because he is the true Messiah, the Son of God, who should save not through war, political initiative or spectacular actions aimed at his own enhancement but through suffering and obedience to God, without reference to any earthly contingency: Jesus for this very reason refuses to come down from the cross. The devil's first and last temptations — in the desert and on the cross — are rejected by Jesus.

An observation

Now that we have reached this point I should like to make one observation about methodology: since this is an academic lecture it is subject to certain limitations, the most serious of which is that it has to be short.

This demands that our exegesis of the texts be very basic: I must avoid many interesting ramifications. The greatest pity is that I cannot discuss the connections between certain episodes in Jesus' life and their Old Testament prefigures and prophecies: yet this is very important for an understanding of Jesus' personality and even for faith in him. The Apostles put a lot of stress on these parallells when preaching to the Jews: St Paul, for example, in preaching to the Jews in Pisidia said:

> "Brethren, sons of the family of Abraham, and those among you that fear God, to us has been sent the message of this salvation. For those who live in Jerusalem and their rulers, because they did not recognize him [Jesus] nor understand the utterances of the prophets which are read every sabbath, fulfilled these by condemning him. Though they could charge him with nothing deserving death, yet they asked Pilate to have him killed. And when they had fulfilled all that was written of him, they took him down from the tree, and laid him in a tomb. But God raised him from the dead; and for many days he appeared to those who came up with him from Galilee to Jerusalem, who are now his witnesses to the people. And we bring you the good news that God promised to the fathers, this he has fulfilled to us their children by raising Jesus; as also it is written in the second psalm, 'Thou are my Son, today I have begotten thee.'" (Act 13:26-33).

Jesus and the State

If, throughout his public ministry Jesus clearly was above
any kind of involvement in earthly affairs, there still can
be gleaned from the Gospels enough material to allow us
discern a consistent attitude on his part towards the State
— which at that time was the Roman Empire; however, the
attitude would seem applicable to any State.

First I should like to point out the Copernican revolution
Jesus introduces into the theocratic view of the State prevalent among Palestinian Jews at the time. For them, the Kingdom of God and the State fuse at the level of the messianic
ideal — an ideal which excludes the existence of any State
other than the Jewish one. The Gentiles will have to submit
to the Messiah, who will conquer them in the eschatological
war. This will bring about the universalism of the Israelite
religion: the nations will come in submission to adore the
God of Israel in Jerusalem; from then on he will be the
God of all the nations. The King of the Jews is Lord's
Anointed, his deputy on earth. The Israelite, as a matter of
principle, will not submit to any State other than his own
theocratic-Jewish one. For Palestinian Judaism of Jesus'
time, the presence of the Roman State was never just a political problem: it was a religious problem and a problem of
conscience. Every Israelite should reject out of hand any
form of submission to the Roman State, on grounds of
religion and conscience. The "publicans", whose job implied a form of collaboration (admittedly indirect) with
those in power, are automatically in the same class as "sinners". This climate of opinion can be noticed often in the
Gospels.

For Jesus, on the other hand — as we shall see — there is
no question of outright rejection of the Roman State; yet
neither is his attitude merely acritical.[50] This means that

he has a definite attitude to the State, which involves establishing spheres of competence, at least on the level of criteria. Putting it in an over-simple way we could say that he establishes two levels of competence: the Roman State is responsible for "temporal affairs", Jesus for "permanent affairs" — i.e. religious, eternal matters.

We must now look at some passages from the Gospel.[51]

The question of tribute to Caesar

This episode is related in the three synoptic Gospels (Mt 22:15-22; Mk 12:13-17; Lk 20:20-26). The three texts are quite parallel and equivalent. We shall follow the Matthew text:

15   Then the Pharisees went and took counsel on how to entangle him in his talk.

16   And they sent their disciples to him, along with the Herodians, saying, "Teacher, we know that you are true and teach the way of God truthfully, and care for no man; for you do not regard the position of men.

17   Tell us, then, what you think. Is it lawful to pay taxes to Caesar, or not?"

18, 19

But Jesus, aware of their malice, said, "Why put me to the test, you hypocrites? Show me the money for the tax". And they brought him a coin.

20   And Jesus said to them "Whose likeness and inscription is this?"

21   They said, "Caesar's". Then he said to them, "Render therefore to Caesar the things that are Caesar's, and to God the things that are God's".

Obviously the Pharisees — for once in agreement with the Herodians — were trying to send Jesus into a blind alley: if he answered yes, there they were, ready to point out to the people that Jesus was a traitor to the cause of Israel. If he answered no, then the Herodians would denounce him as hostile and rebellious to the Roman State. They would, they thought, be able to catch him in a trap. But Jesus leaves them quite perplexed — and yet his reply is not evasive or diplomatic: it has a depth they cannot plumb and yet it is absolutely faithful to the way he has been preaching the Kingdom of God: give Caesar what is his, but nothing more; for indeed we must give God what is his — the necessary other side of the question, though it had not been asked him. They are not on the same level, because for an Israelite God transcends each and every human category. What is it that belongs to Caesar? The payment of taxes, without which no State can operate. What is it that must be given to God? Obviously *all* the commandments, which imply personal love and self-surrender. Jesus' reply reaches much higher than the human horizon of his tempters; it is away above the Yes and No which they want to extract from him. The trap they have laid is quite diabolical for it is really an attempt to reduce Jesus' religious and transcendental attitude to one of involvement in temporal affairs: by becoming either a collaborator with the occupying power, or a revolutionary. The manoeuvre is diabolical because, later on, the Jews will bring a false accusation against him to Pilate: "We found this man perverting our nation, and forbidding us to give tribute to Caesar" (Lk 23:2); and I call it diabolical because lying results from the action of the devil and he is the father of this lie — a lie which eventually is quite barefaced.

Jesus' reply cuts through the God/Caesar antinomy — the counterposing of divine power and human power, Christ's mission and the temporal competence of the State or of civil society. These are questions which operate on different planes: they meet only if they are — illegitimately — forced on to the same plane. The State should not be raised to the level of God — nor should Christ and, therefore, his Church, be lowered to the level of men[52]: doing either one or other of these things leads to Church-State conflict — as is the case in the present example where the Jews tried to get Jesus to "define" himself vis-a-vis the Roman State.

But Jesus' reply is deep and positive: he does not wriggle out of the question: he re-expresses it in the right way and shows the only direction to go in to solve it. Jesus does not confuse the Kingdom of God with the State (this confusion was at the very basis of the Palestinian Judaism of his time and the root of this trick question about payment of tribute to Caesar). On the contrary, Jesus, in locating once more his divine, salvific mission on the plane where it should always be (the religious plane in its noblest sense) sets himself against both the erroneous Jewish concept of political messianism and the wrongful interference of the Roman State (and therefore of any other State) in the sphere of religion.

Jesus reply, we have said, was positive, because in the context of the Roman empire, in which the Emperor is worshipped as a God, Jesus does not recognise this sphere of competence: indeed, when he says "And to God the things that are God's" (Ἀπόδοτε... καὶ τὰ τοῦ Θεοῦ τῷ Θεῷ) — Jesus is clearly stating that there are things which should not be given to Caesar, but rather to God. The Christians of the first centuries with their μαρτυρία, martyr's witness, will be the best exegesis of these words of our Lord: by giving up their lives rather than render divine worship to the Emperor they will practise to an heroic degree this teaching of the Master, — which it was very difficult to practise in their historical situation.

In his reply, Jesus has established once and for all two spheres of competence which previously had not been well defined. The civil institution and the religious should not be confused or absorbed into one another or meddle in each others' personal affairs: they should act in harmony with each other, each respecting the other's sphere. In other words we could say that from this scene we can deduce rejection of the "clerocracy" and of "layocracy". "clerical-ism" or "laicism", using these words in their technical-pejorative strict sense which they have acquired, with time, in the language of Church-State relations.

The dialogue with Pilate

After being questioned in the house of Caiphas, the high priest, Jesus is brought to the praetorium, to be charged before the Roman procurator. Here we will use St John's account (18:29, 33-36):

29 So Pilate went out to them and said, "What accus-ation (κατηγορία) do you bring against this man?"

33 Pilate entered the praetorium again and called Jesus, and said to him, "Are you the King of the Jews? Jesus answered:

34 "Do you say this of your own accord, or did others say it to you about me?"

35 Pilate answered, "Am I a Jew? Your own nation and the chief priests have handed you over to me; what have you done?"

36 Jesus answered, "My kingship is not of this world (ἡ βασιλεία ἡ ἐμὴ οὐκ ἔστιν ἐκ τοῦ τούτου).

If my Kingship were of this world (ἐι ἐκ τοῦ κόσμου τούτου ἦν ἡ βασιλεία ἡ ἐμή...) my servants would fight, that I might not be handed over to the Jews; but my kingship is not from the world (νῦν δὲ ἡ βασιλεία ἡ ἐμὴ οὐκ ἔστιν ἐντεῦθεν). "

Jesus' reply disconcerts Pilate. Here is Jesus on trial; he has been denounced to the procurator so as to get Pilate to use his political authority to condemn him. Pilate has to make sure that Jesus did in fact set himself up as Jewish king, that is to say, whether he really was a nationalist ringleader, or just perhaps a plain criminal. Jesus tries to get him to understand the true nature of his "kingship", and he explains it in Jewish terms but in a way which a Gentile can grasp. He twice says that his kingship is not "of this world" and a third equivalent "from here" (ἐντεῦθεν). I said that he disconcerted Pilate: Jesus had proposed that another lawful sovereignty existed, distinct from that of the Emperor. But not in competition with it, for he had stressed it was not a sovereignty "of this world".

Probably the only thing Pilate grasped was that this man was neither a nationalist rebel nor a criminal — he sensed this from what he said and also from his gestures and the other circumstances of this particular case.

But it should be noticed that this last phrase "my kingdom is not from this world" ('Η βασιλεία ἡ ἐμή οὐκ ἔστιν ἐκ τοῦ κόσμου τούτου) must be understood in the complex biblical concept of "world" = κόσμος = 'Olam, which implies two aspects at one and the same time: the temporal = αἰών = *saeculum* = the age, and the "quasi-spatial" = cosmos. The present material world, which we can see with our eyes, has a limited life-span, el *'olâm hazzéh*, ὁ κόσμος οὗτος 'the present age, which will last until "the end of the world", that is, although it be a tautology, until 'the end of the present age or time", the συντέλεια τοῦ αἰῶνος. Then will come the "saeculum venturum", "the future age or time" or "world to come", the *'olâm ha-ba*, ὁ αἰών ὁ μέλλων.[53] Between the first and the second coming of Christ is the period of transition between the two "times" or "worlds": the world or "present" age receives a death blow through the eruption in it of the future age, after the resurrection of Jesus. It is between the Resurrection and the Parousia that the tension is produced: "already, but not yet", i.e. the future world has begun, but in a very inchoate, very preliminary, way. It does exist, for the risen Jesus already rejoices in the future state of bodily resurrection which awaits us all at the end of this "present world or age". It would have been very difficult for Jesus to get Pilate to understand all this, and more, in that short meeting. Therefore he limits himself to telling him he can be at ease, for his kingdom, strictly speaking, does not belong to this "present world or time". In this world Jesus is not going to exercise his kingship in "temporal" competition with the "kings of the earth". However, their kingship is provisional and temporary: it will last only as long as this present world, whereas Jesus' will be absolute and eternal in the same way as the "future time or world" will be eternal.

The trial of Jesus

He is questioned in the presence of the chief priests

12 So the band of soldiers and their captain and the officers of the Jews seized Jesus and bound him.

13 First they led him to Annas (Jn 18:12-13).

We should note that the arrest is an official affair, it is made on the authority of the Romans, for otherwise the presence of the captain and his cohort could not have occurred.

The interview at the house of Annas, however, has no official character at all. Annas is not the high priest; he has only a moral influence in the city. Besides, Annas questions Jesus in a very cursory manner and perhaps very briefly "about his disciples and his teaching" (Jn 18:19), and Jesus limits his reply to saying that he had spoken in public and therefore had nothing to add to what he had so often said in the synagogue and in the temple (Jn 18:20-21). Annas sent him to the high priest Caiphias (Jn 18:24), where the scribes and elders had gathered (Mt 26:57; Mk 14:38).

Neither did the questioning that took place at the house of Caiphas have the formality of a proper legal process aimed at handing down sentence: its purpose was to establish certain charges so that Jesus could be denounced to the Roman procurator.

In other words, Caiphas knew that the Romans would only be interested in questions of public order i.e. civil or political crimes. Pilate would take an interest in the affair only if he were offered more or less convincing evidence that Jesus was projecting himself as a zealot-style messiah, i.e. as a nationalistic leader. This must be why the high priest formulates his key question: "I adjure you by the living God, tell us" (Mt 26:63)– Σὺ εἰ ὁ Χριστὸς ὁ Υἱὸς τοῦ Εὐλογητοῦ,

"Are you the Christ, the Son of the Blessed? (Mk 14:61)
-- Σὺ εἶ ὁ Χριστός ὁ Υἱὸς τοῦ Εὐλογητοῦ,
"tell us if you are the Christ, the Son of God" (Mt 26:63).
– Σὺ εἶ ὁ Χριστός ὁ Υἱὸς τοῦ Θεοῦ;
"if you are the Christ, tell us" (Lk 22:67).
– Εἰ σὺ εἶ ὁ Χριστός, εἰπὸν ἡμῖν

Caiphas thinks he has cornered Jesus. His question is not backed by any readiness to believe in Jesus (that is quite obvious); he wants to create a fatal dilemma for him. If Jesus answered No to being the Messiah he would be completely discredited in the eyes of the people: he would be seen as a coward who recanted at the moment of decision out of fear of death. If he answered Yes, he was the Messiah, he would have to give the Jews some spectacular proof of it and in any event he would be in rebellion against Caesar, or so the Romans would see it.

St John has not given us Caiphas' question. The three synoptics have, but with the three different nuances which I have transcribed.

But Jesus, knowing Caiphas' intention, replies by raising the question onto a new plane. What Matthew in fact gives us is a literal Greek translation of the Aramaic:

Σὺ εἶπας: You have said so (Mt 26:64). Luke gives a more long-winded description: "If I tell you, you will not believe; and if I ask you you will not answer" (Lk 22:67-68): this is probably an interpreted *explanation* rather than a transcription of Jesus' exact reply.

Finally, Mark leaves us somewhat disconcerted by transcribing:Εγώ εἰμι "I am" (Mk 14:62).

Most modern critics think that Matthew's version is the most exact and literal reply, for a number of reasons but mainly because of the Aramaic and concise structure of the reply according to Matthew which would put the accent on the "you" and would constitute an evasive way of dealing with an incorrect question: it would amount to saying: "You say so, not I" or rather "You will see", as Luke 22: 67-68 explains.

The reply in Mk 14:62 is not as disconcerting as it at first appears: it fits the situation perfectly, for Jesus does not stop here: he immediately goes on to say, "You will see the Son of man sitting at the right hand of Power (= God), and coming with the clouds of heaven" (Mt 26:64; Mk 14:62; Lk 22:69). Here Jesus once again wishes to show that his messianism is not the messianism of the nationalistic King: it is the transcendental messianism which Daniel 7:13 foretold; in other words, Jesus declares he is Son of God, which means Messiah, but not of the Jewish nationalistic type. Perhaps the High Priest did not expect this second part of the reply; but showing great quickness of mind and sense of drama, he "tore his robes, and said, 'He has uttered blasphemy. Why do we still need witnesses? You have now heard his blasphemy. What is your judgment'? They answered, 'He deserves death'" (Mt 26:65-66; cf. Mk 14:63-64; Lk 22:71). Once again Jesus avoids naively stating his messianism; he is waiting for the time when such a statement can be combined with stressing the transcendental character of his messiahship.

But what is most surprising is that this meeting with the chief priest, scribes and elders ought to have led to Jesus being condemned to death by stoning: they had the power to do this, as we will see a few years later when St Stephen is martyred (Acts 7:54-60), without getting into difficulties with the Roman authorities. But: what about the people? The Pharisees and elders already wanted to get rid of Jesus, but they had not dared to do so for fear of the people's reaction.[54] What they were aiming at, as I have said, was to establish the basis for a *denunciation* of Jesus to the procurator: they wanted the people to see the Roman authorities "taking responsibility" for Jesus' death. The interrogation had not followed the course the priests expected: Jesus had not "compromised" himself by opting in any "temporal" or political direction. Perhaps this is what most exasperated them.

And, in the final analysis, since their aim was not to seek the truth but to have Jesus condemned, they mixed the divine with the human. Jesus, once again, had said No to nationalistic messianism: his mission was divine, he was the Son of God. The priests, lying in the way Satan lied, turned the thing on its head: they used Jesus' statement that he was Son of God (transcendental messianism) to denounce him as a political plotter against Caesar.[55]

Once the charade was over, they brought him to the Roman procurator.

The trial before Pilate

> Jn 18:28a: Then they led Jesus from the house of Caiphas to the praetorium.

> Lk 23:2-5: And they began to accuse him, saying, "We found this man perverting our nation, and forbidding us to give tribute to Caesar, and saying that he himself is Christ a King".

These texts need no commentary. The treachery of the chief priests, elders and scribes is quite obvious (cf. Mk 15:1; Mt 27:1-2); they totally misrepresent Jesus and denounce him to the Roman procurator as a political subversive and rebel. Pilate evidently is not aware of the religious dimension of the concept of Messiah: but it is his job to keep public order and maintain Casear's authority in this province of the empire. Therefore, in line with the charges, Pilate's first question is inevitable; the three Synoptics all report it word for word:

> "Are you the King of the Jews?" ($- \Sigma\grave{v}\ \epsilon\tilde{\iota}\ \grave{o}\ \beta\alpha\sigma\iota\lambda\epsilon\grave{v}\varsigma$ $\tau\tilde{\omega}\nu\ \text{'}Iou\delta\alpha\acute{\iota}\omega\nu$;): Mt 27:11; Mk 15:2; Lk 23:3).

Although it is a natural question for Pilate to ask, it is difficult to reply to it. Jesus answers: "You have said so" ($\Sigma\grave{v}\ \lambda\acute{\epsilon}\gamma\epsilon\iota\varsigma$). — exactly the same in the three Synoptics. We have already referred, when Jesus was questioned at Caiphas' (cf. Mt 26:64; Lk 22:67-68), to the meaning of his similar reply "You say so" ($\Sigma\grave{v}\ \epsilon\tilde{\iota}\pi\alpha\varsigma$). now the reply is in the present tense. To understand what this reply means you have to situate it in the context of the different meanings it had for Pilate, for the Jews themselves, and for Jesus. It is a *nuanced* reply; it uses an ambiguous Aramaic turn of phrase, not because Jesus wants to give a dissimulating reply but because a simple straight reply would not convey exactly the *way* he was king.

As on many other occasions, St John's Gospel fills in the gaps in the Synoptics:

John 18:28-34:

> Then they led Jesus from the house of Caiphas to the praetorium. It was early. They themselves did not enter the praetorium, so that they might not be defiled, but might eat the passover.

29 So Pilate went out to them and said, "What accusation to you bring against this man?"

30 They answered him, "If this man were not an evildoer, we would not have handed him over".

31 Pilate said to them, "Take him yourselves and judge him by your own law". The Jews said to him, "It is not lawful for us to put any man to death".

32 This was to fulfil the word which Jesus had spoken to show what death he was to die.

33 Pilate entered the praetorium again and called Jesus, and said to him:

34 "Are you the King of the Jews?" Jesus answered "Do you say this of your own accord, or did others say it to you about me?"

Before giving his qualified answer Jesus, as always, wants to leave the apolitical character of his mission perfectly clear. It is worth stressing this: the consistency of Jesus' attitude to the spiritual nature of his mission, from beginning to end of his public ministry. And St John goes on:

> Jn 18:35: Pilate answered, "Am I a Jew? Your own nation and the chief priests have handed you over to me; what have you done? "

Pilate does not change the course of his examination; he continues to approach the case from the point of view of public law and order; his questions are aimed at seeing if the charges against Jesus are justified: Do you want to become king? Are you a criminal? Jesus tries to make Pilate understand what his mission really is, and he explained it in terms which a Gentile could most easily understand.

> Jn 18:36: Jesus answered: "My kingship is not of this

world; if my kingship were of this world my servants would fight, that I might not be handed over to the Jews; but my kingship is not from this world".

Pilate does not know what to make of the reply: is there another legitimate sovereignty, distinct from that of the Emperor? No. Yet this man xxxxxxxx, for he speaks of "another world". The Procurator tries to steer the conversation back to his own area of competence:

John 18:37: "So you are a king? "

And Jesus tries again to get him to understand the special nature of his "kingship":

John 18:37: "You say that I am a king. For this I was born, and for this I have come into the world, to bear witness to the truth. Every one who is of the truth hears my voice."

Jesus persists in his attitude, bringing the question back on to his own plane. Obviously Pilate cannot grasp all this: "King of another world; bearing witness to the truth ... " But from his point of view — that of a politician — he does realise that all this is outside his competence:

John 18:38: Pilate said to him, "What is truth? " After he had said this, he went out to the Jews again, and told them, "I find no crime in him".

The words which St John puts in Pilate's mind a little later (19:12) could apply at this particular point: "Upon this Pilate sought to release him" In other words, Pilate probably had realised three things: (1) That this man was innocent of any political or civil crime; (2) that the whole affair was outside his sphere: it was a religious matter, over which he had no jurisdiction; (3) that the Jews' accusations were a cock and bull story in which they wanted to get him involved. The chief priests and scribes had already foreseen this in some way, but with diabolical treachery they now endeavour to switch the basis of their accusation of Jesus from religious grounds to civil, political grounds. And I say diabolical, because this stubborn attitude of the members of the Sanhedrin is consistent with the devil's effort to "tempt" Jesus from the very beginning of his public ministry: Jesus keeps freeing himself of these nets which would make his a temporalist mission — but Satan keeps on throwing the same nets at him.

And now comes Pilate's political but cowardly manoeuvring. Jesus is innocent, but the Jews are at a high pitch. So he now starts going the way of concessions: first, the application of the paschal amnesty. But it fails: "Not this man, but Barabbas". No success, either, comes from referring the matter to Herod Antipas, when he learns that Jesus comes from Galilee and therefore is subject, in the first instance, to Herod. His third effort is to appeal to the Jews' compassion:

Lk 23:13-16

13   Pilate then called together the chief priests and the rulers and the people,

14   and said to them, "You brought me this man as one who was perverting the people; and after examining him before you, behold, I did not find this man guilty of any of your charges against him,

15   neither did Herod, for he sent him back to us. Behold, nothing deserving death has been done by him;

16   I will therefore chastise him and release him.

John 19:1-6:

1   Then Pilate took Jesus and scourged him.

2   And the soldiers plaited a crown of thorns, and put it on his head, and arrayed him in a purple robe;

3   they came up to him, saying, "Hail, King of the Jews!" and struck him with their hands.

4   Pilate went out again, and said to them, "Behold, I am bringing him out to you, that you may know that I find no crime in him".

5   So Jesus came out, wearing the crown of thorns and

the purple robe. Pilate said to them, "Here is the man!"

6   When the chief priests and the officers saw him, they cried out, "Crucify him, crucify him! "

We can now see what a bad psychologist Pilate is: he knows nothing about pseudo-religious fanaticism. Those people had decided to give their hatred full vent (a satanic hatred, surely) and they are hardened in their cruelty! They resort to lies and inconsistencies to get the Procurator to condemn Jesus: at first (Jn 19:7) they allege, "We have a law, and by that law he ought to die, because he has made himself the Son of God". But that is not the Procurator's business, so they then accuse him of political crime:

John 19:12:

"If you release this man, you are not Caesar's friend; everyone who makes himself a king sets himself against Caesar". When Pilate heard these words, he brought Jesus out and sat down on the judgment seat at a place called The Pavement, and in Hebrew, Gabbatha.

Now they have got what they want. Pilate is afraid of what these fanatics might do to him (they could even denounce him) so he formally decides to judge Jesus for a political crime; he feels absolute disgust for them and plans — as a cowardly revenge — to humiliate them as much as he can.

John 19:14-15:

He said to the Jews, "Here is your King!"

15   They cried out, "Away with him, away with him, crucify him! " Pilate said to them, "Shall I crucify your King? " The chief priests answered, "We have no king but Caesar".

They have reached the summit of lying and ignomINY: any means whatever are permitted provided they get the political powers-that-be to eliminate their religious enemy

— and they pull it off. They have managed to compromise the Roman State in a religious matter, even against the will of the legal representative of the Empire. Truly, as Jesus put it earlier, when he was arrested in Gethsemani: "This is your hour, and the power of darkness" (Lk 22:53): Jesus has been turned over, for a few hours, to hidden satanic powers, whose weapons are always the same — falsehood, lies, confusion, and ultimately the condemnation of the people they used as their tools: for at the trial of Jesus it was those Jews and Pilate himself who were really judged and found guilty:

Mt 27:24:

> So when Pilate saw that he was gaining nothing, but rather that a riot was beginning, he took water and washed his hands before the crowd, saying, "I am innocent of this righteous man's blood; see to it yourselves".
>
> 25 And all the people answered, "His blood be on us and on our children!"

Mk 15:15:

> So Pilate, wishing to satisfy the crowd, released for them Barabbas; and having scourged Jesus, he delivered him up to be crucified.

The Gospel accounts are extremely explicit in showing the various attitudes of the leaders of the priests and of Pilate: no commentary is called for. Here is another example of satanic obstinancy. And so the trial before the Roman procurator comes to an end and for political reasons a sentence of death is handed down:

> Pilate also wrote a title (sentence) and put it on the cross; it read, "Jesus of Nazareth, the King of the Jews" (Jn 19:19).

Conclusion

To conclude this essay it should not be necessary to stress that throughout his public ministry Jesus has a constant policy of *teaching*, on the one hand, the transcendence of his saving mission as Messiah and the Son of God; while on the other he *defended* that transcendence repeatedly and from every possible angle, against any attempt to "temporalize" this religious mission. In other words, we have seen him reject temporal dominion over "the kingdoms of this world"[56] — and reject also political action aimed at defending the Jewish national cause against Roman domination;[57] he does not even accept the title and role of the King-Messiah as understood by most Palestinian Jews of his time[58], nor will he allow himself be used as judge in legal questions such as the division of legacies.[60]

He rejected all this as a satanic temptation aimed at reducing his religious-salvific mission to a temporal activity (however noble that might be in its own sphere). How could anyone reject the validity of the Jewish nationalist movement aimed at political independence, for example? The gospel texts we have considered show us that Jesus saw himself, very very often, under external pressure of different kinds to "reduce" his mission to the temporal level: but that he always rejected these pressures.

On the other hand, it is an article of faith that the Church is the instrument which Jesus uses in order to do his work of salvation. The Church's mission is a share in Christ's mission (cf. Mt 28:18-20). This mission of Christ and his Church consists in offering men God's salvation, leading them to their eternal and supernatural destiny, to freedom from sin, and having them share in the very being and life of the Blessed Trinity (cf. 2 Pt 1:4). To say it in a few words, we can state with certainty that the Church's activity is a religious activity which occurs mainly through the ministry of the evangelical word and through the sacraments[61] which are — taken together — a sharing in the salvific power of the human nature of the risen Christ: the strength of Christ the head passes through the Church, his body.[62]

It should be clear that when I speak of the Church, I am referring strictly to the Church *qua talis*, as such, as Body of Christ, as the society which administers the goods of salvation. Christians in so far as they are men and women, citizens of this world, are something else. In this world they have an obligation and a right to act as the kind of people they are — "committing themselves in temporal action" in search of solutions to social, political, cultural, artistic, professional and other questions. But it is obvious (or at least it should be) that in this case they are acting as men and women, as citizens, and in no way as representatives, either official or unofficial, of the Church.

In this we children of the Church have full freedom, we are quite untrammelled, but at the same time we have a serious moral obligation to ensure that the principles and the kind of earthly structures and methods we propose do not go against revealed doctrine but, quite the contrary, are infused with its values.[63] We have seen how Jesus admitted to his group of disciples men from different tendencies and that he never discussed with them their opinions or options in earthly affairs. In fact, he did not even forbid them carrying a sword: what he prohibited was the use of the sword in the supreme moment of his arrest in Gethsemani.

We have demonstrated that Jesus was not a temporal messiah. It would take us further than this lecture to show that this conclusion, which our exegesis has led us to, constitutes a truth of faith, taught by the magisterium, which affects the very being and life of the Church itself. I am excluding, then, from my study concrete historical and theological nuances which refer to the transcendental character of the Church's mission in so far as it is the continuer of Christ's mission.

I am not trying here to move (theologically speaking) from the public behaviour of Jesus to the public and official attitude of the Church. That is a large and delicate subject which would call for a special though complementary study which I have not taken on and do not have time to take on here.

Therefore, I am not going to discuss the concrete ways Jesus' attitude to the politics of his nation should affect the way the Church acts over the whole spectrum of differend political situations in different countries at different points in history. Indeed, I am not even going to refer to the role the Church, as such, may or may not have in the ordering of temporal affairs.

Vatican Council II, in continuity with all the previous magisterium, has underlined the essentially religious mission of the Church, which transcends all possible temporal options: in these options the Church should not involve itself.[64] It has also shown that — with an eye to the common good and to the shaping of human social life in a manner which facilitates man on his earthly way towards his ultimate goal, God — the Church can and sometimes must make high-level moral-religious judgments regarding these structures and shapes of the earthly city.[65]

However, from our short essay (not corroborated by a parallel theological study of the texts of the magisterium), it seems easy to deduce that the Church, in so far as it is Christ's body is, like its Lord, above ideologies, political regimes, social movements, pressure groups, parties, professional and national bodies etc., while still being deeply interested in and concerned about these human affairs although from a lofty perspective.

But all these things, all these very often noble human affairs, are still ephemeral and changeable. What was at one time regarded as being an important social advance, for example, as *the* final stage of a long process, becomes absolutely a thing of the past. All this is, then, unstable and changing. Christ, the Church, are on the other hand eternal, just as their mission is eternal. It can sometimes happen as happened with Jesus when almost abandoned on the cross: he seemed to have failed, precisely by not opting for one of the possible human solutions: neither the Jews nor the Romans followed him. But no: it was exactly the opposite: Jews and Romans, Greeks and barbarians, freemen and slaves, men and women, healthy and sick, all begin to follow this God become man, who has freed us from sin, to set out for an eternal destiny, where alone will emerge the true fulfilment and freedom of man, made in the image and likeness of God, and whose deepest aspiration far exceeds any passing activity, however noble it may be. Is not this — and nothing less than this — what mankind and every single individual ask of and even require of the Church? Is not this and nothing less than this the mission Christ entrusted to his Church?

1. Seutonius, *Caligula,* 32; *Domitian,* 10. Dion Casius, 54, 8. The *titulus* could also be written on a board hung round the neck of the condemned person: this was done, for example, in the case of the martyrs of Lyons, according to Eusebius, *Historia Ecclesiastica* V, I, 44. The INRI on Jesus' cross is an example of the Evangelists' historical accuracy: this is the opinion of such non-Catholic critics as H. Lietzmann ("Der Prozess Jesu" in *Sitzungsberichte der Deutschen Akademie der Wissenschaften,* Berlin, 1931, 313ff.), M. Dibelius ("Das historische Problem der Leidensgeschichte" in *Zeitschrift fur die neutestamentliche Wissenschaft und die Kunde der altern Kirche* 1930, 200), E. Dinkler ("Petrusbekennetnis und Satanswort, Das Problem der Messianitat Jesu" in *Zeit und Geschichte: Dankesgabe an R. Bultmann,* 1964, 148), O. Cullmann (*Jesus y los revolucionarios de su tiempo,* Madrid 1971, 50) and many others. However, although it comes as no surprise, R. Bultmann is of the opinion that the historicity of the INRI should be rejected, but he offers no scholarly argument for this view (cf. R. Bultmann, *Geschichte der synoptischen Tradition,* 3rd ed., 1961, 293).

2. This is not my idea: it is to be found *passim* in the works of certain contemporary exegetes.

3. On these matters and in general on the religious, political, social situation of Palestinian Judaism at the time of Jesus cf. the learned study by E. Schurer, *Geschichte des judischen Volkes im Zeitalter Jesu Christ,* 3 vols, Leipsig 1901-1909 and the extension of this work by J. Jeremias, *Jerusalem zur Zeit Jesu,* Gottingen 1958. As regards religious beliefs and institutions cf. J. Bonsirven, *Le judaisme palestinien an temps de Jesus-Christ,* 2 vols, Paris 1935.

4. This synthetic idea is not mine: it is today the common patrimony of biblical scholars.

5. On Old Testament conceptions of messianic restoration cf. *Manual Biblico,* a collective work, Madrid 1967, vol. II, 422-467.

6. Cf. P. Grelot, *Sentido cristiano del Antiguo Testamento,* Bilbao 1967.

7. Cf. mainly: A. Gelin, "Messianisme" in *Supplement au Diction-naire de la Bible*, Paris 1957, vol. V. cols 1165-1212; M.J. Lagrange, *Le messianisme chez les Juifs*, Paris 1909; J. Drummond, *The Jewish Messiah*, London 1877; J. Bonsirven, *Le judaisme palestinien au Temps de Jesus-Christ*, vol. I, Paris 1934; Idem, *Les idees juives au Temps de Notre-Seigneur*, Paris 1933; H. Shalin, *Der Messias und das Gottesvolk*, Uppsala 1945; Elfers, *Reich Gottes einst und jetzt*, Pad-erborn 1948; U. Pisanelli, *Il segreto Messianico nel vangelo di S· Marco*, Rovigo 1953; R Buchheim, *Das messianische Reich. Uber den Usprung der Kirche im Evangelium*, Munich 1949; P. Volz, *Die eschatologie der judischen Gemeinde im neutestamentlichen Zeital-ter*, 2nd edn, 1934, 173ff.; A Bentzen, *King and Messiah*, 1954; J. Coppens, *Le Messianisme royal*, Paris 1968.

8. "Christ . . . on rising from the dead sent his life-giving Spirit upon his disciples and through this Spirit has established his body, the Church, as the universal sacrament of salvation (ut universale salutis sacramentum)": Vatican II, Const. Dogm. *Lumen gentium*, n. 48.

9. In addition to the bibliography suggested in footnote 7 above, there is a great deal of information in S. Mowinckel, *He that cometh: the Messiah concept in the O.T. and later Judaism*, Oxford 1957, Cf. also M. Revuelta, *Enemigos de Cristo*, Bilbao 1960; G.F. Moore, *Juda-ism in the first centuries of the Christian era*, 3 vols, Cambridge, Mass., 1927-1930; S.W. Baron, *Histoire d'Israel, vie sociale et religieuse*, Paris 1957.

10. Cf. M. Garcia Cordero, "Expectacion mesianico" in *Enciclope-dia de la Biblia* ed. A. Diez-Macho and S. Bartino, vol. III, Barcelona 1963, cols 381-387; L. Dennefeld, 'Messianisme' in *Dictionnaire de Theologie Catholique*, vol. X, cols 1404-1468; J. Schildenberger, "Weissagung und Erfullung" in *Biblica* 13 (1943), 107-124.

11. In this connection cf. *passim* in J.B. Colon, "La conception du salut d'apres les Evangiles Synoptiques", en *Rev. scien. relig.* 10 (1930), 189-217; 370-415; II (1931), 27-70; 194-223; 382-432.

12. For a survey of the radical rationalist position of J. Wellhausen, see his *Israelitische und judische Geschichte*, 3rd ed., Berlin 1897.

13. E. Sellin did very productive research into all aspects of the Old Testament. His main works (non-radical historicist in tendency) touching on biblical Messianism are *Geschichte des israelitische-judi-schen Volkes*, Freiburg i. Br. 1899; *Die alttestamentliche Religion im Rahmen der andern altorientalischen Religionen*. Leipzig 1901; *Israel-tisch-judische Religionsgerschichte*, Leipzig 1933; *Theologie des AT*, Leipzig 1933.

14. The very exhaustive study (already referred to) by L. Denne-feld, "Messianisme" in *DTC* X, 1404-1567, surveys the state of re-

search into Biblical messianism up to 1928: Cf. especially cols 1535-1543 for an account of the various theories and the methods used.

15. In trying to get an overview of the subject of messianism in the Old Testament I was greatly helped by a long conversation with my colleague, Prof. V. Vegazo, of the Faculty of Theology of the University of Navarre. The reader will find an excellent summary in the article on 'Messianisme' by A. Gelin cited in note 7 above.

16. Cf., just as examples: Mt 9:27; 12:23; 15:22; 21:9; 21:15; Mk 10:47-48; Lk 18:38; Rom 1:3; 2 Tim 2:8.

17. For a short, basic but very good summary of the history of the chosen people from the viewpoint of salvation, cf. P. de Surgy's little book, *Las Grandes etapas del misterio de la salvacion*, Barcelona 1965.

18. Cf. J. Lesetre, "Messie" in *Dictionnaire de la Bible*, ed. F. Vigouroux, IV, col. 1033.

19. 1 Sam 9:16; 24:7; etc.

20. Cf. Ex 28:41.

21. Cf. 1 Kings 19:16.

22. Cf. Is 45:1. Cf. also E. Jenni, "Die Rolle des Kyrios bei Deutero-jesaja" in *THZ* (1954) 241ff.

23. The bibliography on this is vast. We shall offer only a short list of the more important and comprehensive works. Later we shall give other references dealing with sub-divisions of the subject. Cf. E. Schurer, *Geschichte ...*, op. cit. (English version *A History of the Jewish People in the time of Jesus Christ*, 5 vols, Edinburgh 1886-1890): still very useful despite its age; U. Holzmeister, *Historia aetatis Novi Testamenti*, 2nd ed., *Storia dei tempi del NT*, Turin 1950; W. Foerster, *Neu-testamentliche Zeitgeschichte, I: Der zeitgeschichtliche Histergrund des Lebens und der Verkundigung Jesu*, Berlin 1940; R. H. Pfeiffer, *History of NT. Times* with an introduction to the *Apocrypha*, New York 1949; F.M. Abel, *Histoire de la Palestine depuis la conquete d'Alexandre jusqu'a l'invasion arabe*, 2nd ed., 2 vols, Paris 1952; C.K. Barret, *The New Testament Background: Selected Documents*, London 1957; J. Jeremias, *Jerusalem zur Zeit Jesu. Kulturgeschichte*, Leipzig 1923-1937; E. Barker, *From Alexander to Constantine. Passages and Documents illustrating the History of Social and Political Ideas*, Oxford 1956.

24. The main collection of sources for the apocryphal books are: E. Kautsch, *Die Apocryphen und Pseudepigraphen des AT.*, 2 vols, Tubingen 1920; R. H. Charles, *The Apocrypha and Pseudepigrapha of the O.T.*, Oxford 1913; Klostermann-Harnack, *Apocryphen*, 4 vols, Berlin 1903-1929; M. R. James, *The Lost Apocrypha of the O.*

T., London 1920. Cf. also J. B. Frey, "Apocriphes de l'AT", en *Dictionnaire de la Bible, Supplement*, ... Vigouroux, vol. 1, cols 354-360.

25. On Judaic messianism in the time of Jesus, in addition to the works cited in notes 7 and 23, cf. J. Bonsirven, *Le Judaisme pales-tinien au temps de Jesus-Christ*, 2 vols, Paris 1924; J. Coppens, "L'esperance messianique. Les origines et son developpement" in *Rev. Sc. Rel* (1963), 113-149; W.D. Davies, "The Jewish Background of the Teaching of Jesus: Apocalyptic and Pharisaism" in *Expos. Tim.* (1948), 233ff.; L. Dennefeld, *Le Messianisme*, Paris 1929; Idem, "Messianisme" in *DTC*, Paris 1928, 1404-1568; J.B. Frey, "Le conflit entre le messianisme de Jesus et le messianisme des Juifs de son temps". in *Biblica* XIV (1933), 133-149 and 269-292; A. Gelin "Messianisme" in *DBS*, Paris 1955, cols 1165-1222; H.Gressman, *Der Messias*, Gottingen 1929; J. Klausner, *The Messianic idea in Israel*, London 1956; M. J. Lagrange, *Le messianisme chez les Juifs*, Paris 1909; Idem, *Le judaisme avant Jesus-Christ*, Paris 1931; L'Attente du Messie, in *Recherches Bibliques*, Paris 1954; R.E. Brown, "The Messianisme of Qumran" in *Messianism*, published by the *Cath. Bibl. Quat* 1957, 53-82; S. Mowinckel, *He that Cometh*, Oxford 1957; W.D.E. Desterley, *The evolution of the Idea of the Messiah*, New York 1963; P. van Bergen, "L'Attente du Messie" in *Lumiere et Vie* 1958, 1-11; J. Viteau, *Les Psaumes de Salomon*, Paris 1911.

26. For a good resume of "messianic hope" in Jesus' time see A. Robert y A. Tricot, *Iniciacion Biblica*, Mexico 1957, 706-709. Cf. also J. Coffens, "L'esperance messianique", in *Revue des Sciences Religieuses* 87 (1963) 118-149 y 225-248. Our quotation from Psalm 17 are taken from R. H. Charles' translation in the edition cited in note 24 above (a few very minor changes have been made).

27. Cf. these words of the Jewish Dr J. Klausner, as late as 1922, in his book first published in Hebrew in Jerusalem and then in a German translation, Berlin 1930 as *Jesus von Nazareth, seine Zeit, sein Leben und seine Lehre*: "Jesus was, undoubtedly, a Jew; but in both method and content his teaching deviates from Judaism; it had a kind of non-Jewish quality which would sooner or later have led to separation. In addition to this there is Jesus' indifference (scarcely less than absolute) to the unhappy political circumstances the Jewish people found themselves in at that time. Thus, Judaism, unless it were to deny itself and be unfaithful to its best traditions, was obliged to reject the person and teaching of Jesus" (Introduction, p.1).

28. Cf. J.B. Frey, *Le conflit* ... op. cit, 141-148.

29. Cf. these conclusions of the Jewish writer J. Klausner in another book, *Die Messianichen Vorstellungen des judischen Volkes im Zeit-alter der Tannaiten*, Berlin 1904, 119: "The point of departure of the messianic idea was a political perspective — the burning desire to re-

cover lost political power and see the restoration of the Davidic monarchy; that is why, despite all the efforts to spiritualise it and stress its moral character, it had to remain necessarily and essentially political and earthly. The messianic kingdom was, properly speaking, the kingdom of David, but understood in a broad sense, purified and decked out in all kinds of worldly splendour — as much as the oriental imagination could envisage as compatible with its earthly and political character. For the kingdom of the Jewish Messiah is and remains, at least as it was seen from the period of the Tannites forward, a kingdom of this world".

30. We should emphasise that this earthbound political concept of messianism, which Judaism forged at the time of Jesus, and which later Judaism really seized on, was not the legitimate end-product of the purest religious tradition: that tradition which God created through the prophets whom he sent to the people of Israel.

31. Cf. E. Schürer, *Geschichte des judischen Volkes* ... Vol. 1, 1901, 573ff; G. Baumbach, "Zeloten und Sikarier" in *Theologische Literaturzeitung* (1965), 727ff.

32. Cf. M. Revuelta, "Sanedrin", in *Enciclopedia de la Biblia* (Edic. Garriga), Barcelona 1963, vol. VI, cols 466-467.

33. Cf. O. Cullmann, *Jesus y los revolucionarios de su tiempo*, Madrid 1971, 14-19 and bibliography on 14-16.

34. Cf. C. Wau, "Sicario", in *Enciclopedia de la Biblia*, Barcelona 1963, vol. VI, col. 657.

35. Most historians of the period present this view.

36. Cf. (bearing in mind, however, his Calvinist religious position) O. Cullmann, *Saint Pierre, disciple, apotre, martyr: histoire et theologie*, Neuchatel 1952, 17; and his *El Estado en el NT*, Madrid 1966, 30-31.

37. Cf. O. Cullmann, *El Estado en el NT, op. cit.*, 28; Cullmann quotes F.C. Burkitt, *Syriac Forms of NT. Proper Names*, 1912, 5, and relies on him.

38. Cf. C. C. Torrey, "The Name 'Iscariot'" in *Harvard Theological Review* (1943), 52ff., whose thesis does not seem to be valid. On the contrary, O. Cullmann in *El Estado ...*, *op. cit.*, 28-30 holds a view I would share. The more traditional view that *Iskariotes* is a transcription of the Hebrew *'ish-geryyot*, "man from Carioth", still has supporters, though not many: cf. M.D. Rierola, "Iscariote", in *Enciclop. de la Biblia, op. cit.*, IV, 245 and P. Estelrich, "Qeriyyot", in *Enciclop. de la Biblia*, VI, 14. A very complete, learned and balanced study is that by R.B. Halas, *Judas Iscariot*, Washington D.F. 1946.

39. Cf. notes 27 and 29 re the attitude held not so long ago by Dr J. Klausner.

40. Cf. I. Goma Civit, *El Evangelio segun S. Mateo*, vol. I, Madrid 1966, 128-133.

41. Cf. a summary in J.B. Bauer, "Tentacion", in *Diccionario de Teologia Biblica*, Barcelona 1967, cols 1009-1018.

42. St Thomas Aquinas sums up, in a wonderfully concise way, an idea which is a constant feature of Christian tradition: "ea quae in capite sunt gesta, sunt signa eorum quae nos agere debemus": *S. Th.*, q. 1., a. 10.

43. Naturally I am leaving aside the question of the devil's imperfect knowledge of Jesus being truly the natural Son of God, as also the truth of Jesus' incapacity to sin at any time which derives from the hypostatic union. Cf. e.g. Hebr 4:15; St Leo I, *Epist, ad Flavianum:* Dz (= Denzinger-Schonmetzer, *Enchiridion Symbolorum Definitonum et Declarationum*) 293 (Christus adsumsit formam servi sine sorde peccati); Concilium Oecum. Chalcedonense, *Symbolum*: Dz (= Denzinger-Schonmetzer, *Enchiridion Symbolorum Definitionum et Declarationum*) 301 (Christus per omnia nobis similem absque peccato); Concilium Oecum. Constantinopolitanum III, *Definitio*: Dz 554 (per omnia similem nobis absque peccato).

44. Cf. I. Goma, *op. cit.*, 142 and 145.

45. Cf. L. Marchal, "Evangile selon Saint Luc", in *La Sainte Bible*, ed., L. Pirot and A. Clamer, Paris, vol. X, 1950, p. 161, and note on Lk 12, 13-14.

46. We shall not discuss here the question of the impregnation and perfection of the temporal order by the spirit of the Gospel ("spiritu evangelico rerum temporalium ordinem perfundendi et perficiendi"). Cf. Concilium Oecum. Vaticanum II, *Decretum*, "Apostolicam actuositatem" nn. 5, 7, 11-14, 16, 24, 31; *Decretum* "Ad Gentes", n. 15; *Constit. pastoralis*, "Gaudium et spes", nn. 9, 26, 36, 73-75.

47. Of course these views are in no way opposed to the revealed teaching regarding God's intervention in the government of created Things, even in the smallest of our actions: cf. Mt 6:26-32; Lk:24-30).

48. It should be stressed that all the Greek and all the oldest manuscripts give Peter's full reply (Mt 16:16): "You are the Christ, the Son of the living God". This phrase contains, along with confession of Jesus as Messiah, that of his divine sonship. If Peter had said just "You are the Christ", his confession could be reduced to the concept of Messiah widely held among the Jews of the period: this would not have caused Jesus any joy, or caused him to call Peter blessed — and

certainly would not have been due to a revelation from the Father in heaven, Mt 16:17: "And Jesus answered him, 'Blessed are you, Simon Bariona, for flesh and blood has not revealed this to you, but my Father who is in heaven."

49. Despite the special grace of the Father granted to Peter allowing him to see that Jesus was the Son of God (cf. Mt 16:17), Peter has not managed to understand the depth of Jesus' personality. Like the other Apostles he will come to understand it after the Resurrection and Pentecost.

50. Cf. O. Cullmann, *El Estado ...*, *op. cit.,* 15-19. However, some of Cullmann's views (e.g. "the attitude of the first Christians towards the State ... seems to be contradictory...." *op. cit.,* 17) I do not share: Cullmann sees, particularly, a contrast between Rom 13: 1ff., and Rev 14:1ff; but he fails to put the words of the Apocalypse in their true setting — they refer directly to specific persecutions by the Roman State and to the requirement to treat Caesar as a God. These actions do justify the reprehension they receive in Rev, but they cannot be interpreted as an outright rejection of the State as such.

51. Cullmann, *op. cit,* 16, seems to hit the mark when he says that it is absolutely wrong to identify Christian hope with indifference to present, earthly values: rather the strongest impulses to act *in* this world emanate from Christian hope of the End; Christian eschatology does not simply mean "denial of the world"; though neither does it mean "affirmation of the world". But Cullmann does not distinguish between activity of the Church as such and activity of (individual) Christians in the temporal order. To my mind, this distinction is essential if theoretical and practical confusion is to be avoided. We cannot go into this subject any further now; cf. however the texts of the Magisterium reviewed in note 46 above.

52. It should be clear that whenever I refer to the Church in these contexts, I refer to the Church as such, as universal instrument of salvation, and not therefore to Christians as human beings with citizens' rights and duties which they should exercise and fulfil — citizens who should act freely and responsibly in all the different areas of "temporal" action.

53. For a study of the concept of time in the Bible, and its divisions and the terminology used, cf. J.M. Casciaro, "El tiempo y la Historia en San Pablo" in *Atlantida*, II, 12 (Nov.-Dec. 1964), 576-593. Cf. also J. Goitia, "Indicaciones temporales en la escatologia", in *XVI Semana Biblica Espanola*, Madrid 1956, 50-83; O. Cullmann, *Christ et le Temps*, Neuchatel-Paris, 2nd ed., 1957; J. Barr, *Biblical words for Time*, London 1962.

54. Cf. Mt 21:45-46: "When the chief priests and the Pharisees heard his parables, they perceived that he was speaking about them.

But when they tried to arrest him, they feared the multitudes, because they held him to be a prophet." Parallels in Mk 12:12; Lk 20:19.

55. We do not discuss here why the scribes, Pharisees and chief priests came to have such hatred for Jesus. Cf. in this connection J.B. Frey, *Le conflit ....*, *op. cit.*, 2nd part, 280-292. The best documented modern study of the various interrogations and trials at the start of the Passion is probably Josef Blinzler, *El proceso de Jesus* (Spanish translation, Madrid 1968).

56. Cf. Mt 4:8-10; Lk 4:5-8;

57. Cf. Jn 18:33-36; 19:12-15;

58. Cf. Mt 20:20-28; Mk 10:35-45; To these we might add Jn 6:15, an important passage not studied here.

59. Cf. Lk 12:13-14.

60. Cf. Vatican Council II, Pastoral Constitution *Gaudium et spes*, 42.

61. Cf. Vatican II, Decree *Ad Gentes*, 5.

62. Cf. Vatican II, Dogmatic Constitution *Lumen gentium*, n.7.

63. Cf. documents of the Magisterium cited in note 46 above.

64. Cf. Vatican II, Pastoral Constitution *Gaudium et spes*, 76, 42, 58.

65. Cf. Vatican II, *Gaudium et spes*, 41.

BENEDICT BAUR

FREQUENT CONFESSION

This is a classic book. It deals with the practice of 'individual confession with a personal act of sorrow and the intention to amend and make satisfaction . . . , (with) man's right to a more personal encounter with the crucified, forgiving Christ', as Pope John Paul II described it in *Redemptor Hominis.*

More specifically, the Pope has recommended *frequent* confession, re-proposing the teaching of Pius XII in *Mystici Corporis:* 'for a constant and speedy advancement in the paths of virtue We highly recommend the pious practice of frequent Confession, introduced by the Church under the guidance of the Holy Spirit; for by this means we grow in a true knowledge of ourselves and in Christian humility, bad habits are uprooted, spiritual negligence and apathy are prevented, the conscience is purified and the will strengthened, salutary spiritual direction is obtained, and grace is increased by the efficacy of the sacrament itself.'

With a new introduction by Fr S.M. Ferigle